SHORTEN YOUR JOB SEARCH:

Build Confidence, Communicate Your Value and Quickly Land Your New Job

Book Two: **How to Communicate Your Value**

by

Lloyd L. Feinstein

For information about this publication, please contact:

Lloyd Feinstein
Career Marketing Consultants
25 Dawson Lane
Monroe, New Jersey 08831-2660
www.careermarketingforlife.com
609.655.7730
Email: Lloydfeinstein@yahoo.com

Feinstein, Lloyd, 1941
Shorten Your Job Search: build confidence, communicate your value and quickly land your new job / Part 2: How to Communicate Your Value / Lloyd Feinstein

ISBN: 978-0-9915882-1-3

Dedication

Well, I got your attention and you've opened the cover and here we are. My name is Lloyd.

Problems can be solved and that's what we're going to do.

The best way is to find out who you really are, what it is you really want to do, and what you are truly capable of doing…and then, prepare you to be first in line for that life every time.

My career management secrets are all in the following pages and I'll be with you every step of the way to be sure you get it right. If you complete the work of one chapter each week and build it into the new you, the world will meet the new you in 21 weeks to a better life. You can do it faster; some chapters won't take so long. Depending on how positive and passionate you are for a vibrant, satisfying career, you can do it a lot faster. I'll be with you all the way. For a start, what do you want: a job or a career?

I'll be your counselor and your guide.

– Lloyd Feinstein

Forward

Our two-book series helps you do three needed things:

1. Build confidence
2. Describe your value in a way that hiring managers understand, and
3. Get employed fast!

Step by step, the following chapters will lead you through a communications process that defines your expertise and most salable accomplishments while strengthening your confidence, as it prepares you to ace your interviews.

Inside you'll discover easy, common-sense and effective ways to leverage your background and experience to your advantage. Also, I share some great stuff with you. Therefore, my book has wide appeal for those who need assistance with creating a superior resume as well as landing and managing a new position.

I've tried to create a book that will simulate the experience of working with an expert career counselor to help overcome the obstacles that people struggle with—and that keep them from getting where they want to go in their career.

I have been in training and human resources for 19 years with ITT, Bell Telephone Laboratories, Bellevue Hospital Center, Cadence Industries Corp., and Oppenheimer & Co. More important, I have more than 28 years' experience as a full-time career counselor and advisor to more than 7,800 clients—from recent college graduates to company presidents—and representing all industries, including nonprofits and the self-employed. I am the co-author of the award-winning book *Career Changing:The Worry-Free Guide* published by Little, Brown & Co. (Check out my LinkedIn profile and website, www.careermarketingforlife.com, for further details.)

This book represents the powerful results of all the trial-and-error and give-and-take that thousands of career professionals like you have experienced. These powerful concepts and proven solutions applied by my clients will be presented throughout the book via real-life examples, practical advice, tips, and application of my communication methods.

Enough about me. Let's talk about you. Our game plan starts by first defining the product—YOU (Book One), which is then expanded in this book.

Illustration by Ed Wexler

Next, we define the customer needs. We then match your relevant experience to those needs, develop your marketing materials (including the **marketing resume**), and communicate your **value** via resume, cover and marketing letters to hiring executives. Everything we do in constructing the resume will be fully illustrated and explained. Next we'll cover the basic mechanics of job search, with an emphasis on writing directly to employers. Finally, we'll review how best to interview for the position and close the sale.

Use this book two ways:

1. Obtain an in-depth **understanding** of how the job market works, especially the **hiring process** and its implication for the construction of your resume, as well as how to manage the in-person interview process.

2. Construct a resume that will give you a **competitive advantage** when answering ads to recruiters and headhunters during the interview and closing process.

Though it is possible to skip around the chapters, it is highly recommended that you clearly understand how the job market functions before jumping to those sections that represent your specific situation.

The wide variety of job-search problems makes it difficult to address every possible type of situation, so I've tried to focus on the most common job-search issues.

Employees in all industries and nonprofits will benefit from this book, including:

- line employees trying to move into a management position
- out-of-work employees, regardless of their length of unemployment
- senior executives attempting to reinvigorate their careers
- college graduates trying to establish themselves in a career path
- civilian and military personnel re-entering the job market; and
- entrepreneurs attempting to build their customer bases.

The very fact that you've purchased this book tells me that you're serious about moving your career forward. You don't have to worry. I've been there, on both sides of the hiring desk, and it's going to be OK because my books will show you how to **play the job game to win**.

Preface

Since the current financial crisis, the familiar methods of job search are no longer prudent. Today, we need new strategies and methods to allow you to **stand out from the crowd, demonstrate your value**, and **show how you will fit in.**

Let's begin:

How Do You Evaluate the Information You Hear or Read?

Job search career-management books and articles are full of misinformation, erroneous conclusions, self-serving opinions and every kind of claptrap imaginable. Therefore, how do you **evaluate** what you hear or read?

Answer: Compare what you hear or read against your own reason, common sense and experience!

Here's a gift. Since this book will coach you in ways to meet the hiring executive's needs rather than Human Resources' requirements, give yourself a gift. See how worthwhile these methods and advice are, and how this information makes sense, based on **your own experience**.

* * *

STORY:
How Can a Company Advertise for a Candidate with an MBA and Wind Up Hiring an Individual Without Even an Associate Degree?

Some years ago I counseled a customer-service manager from the technology group of a large bank supporting the brokerage industry. After completing this client's marketing resume, I noticed an ad for a product manager at a small software-development firm. The requirements closely matched my client's background and experience. I answered the ad using a "blind" version of his resume, one that did not identify the person or his employer by name. He got the interview and subsequently was hired into the position, despite the fact that the ad said "MBA preferred." My client had only 50 credits (an associate degree requires 60 credits).

What's going on here? How can a company advertise for a MBA and end up hiring a candidate who has only 50 credits and no degree? I didn't have an answer to this riddle until a few years later, when I came across an article by Pamela Bayless in *Crain's New York Business* titled "Audacity, Charisma Boost Matchmaker." The matchmaker in the article explained how she achieved successful matches between individuals looking for long-term relationships. She said: "People know what they want but not what they need. We give them what they need; they forget what they want."

So the explanation to my query turned out to be simple. The software-development company knew what it wanted and put it in the help-wanted ad. But it was my candidate's marketing resume that represented what the company actually needed—experience, skills and the ability to **fit**. So much so, the company forgot that it wanted a candidate with an MBA.

* * *

Key issue: You don't need more education or certification. What you need is **presentation**—in your resume, and during the interview process.

My books will teach you **presentation skills** and, in the process, guide you through the development of a marketing resume that satisfies **the three universal issues all hiring managers require** (see Chapter 2). In addition, the books will teach you **personal selling skills** that will guide you to change jobs easily when necessary, ace all future performance reviews, and illustrate how best to promote your career. (You will only accomplish these goals, however, by proceeding step-by-step through each chapter in sequence.) If, however, you're ill-prepared for the new world of job search, you run the risk of alienating the very people you want to attract—recruiters, hiring managers and executives.

* * *

What's inside? Take a look at the Contents.

Book Two: **How to Communicate Your Value**

Table of Contents

any hiring manager's three critical issues: are you able to do the job, do you have the necessary experience to solve their problems, and will you fit into the group?

Chapter 7: Why Homework Assignments?
If you're going to be first-team, you need to practice, practice, practice.

Sixteen elements are presented in three main areas of the homework assignment. All are reviewed in detail. List 1: Areas of Expertise / Skill Set; List 2: Describe yourself via 360°feedback from co-workers, and List 3: past work experience in the storytelling format (Problem–Action–Result).

Chapter 8: How Do I Analyze My Resume?
You start with the market—not with you. What does it want that you'd be happy to sell?

This chapter presents the arguments supporting the unorthodox layout of the "marketing resume" and introduces the only two transferable skills *which don't require additional written verification.*

Chapter 9: Valid Transferable Skills Will Beat the Competition.
How to identify and apply them in new ways.

How presentation over education and/or certification is reviewed. What you are up against during a job search is discussed in areas of expertise/skill set and how to define them: the key to resume credibility.

Chapter 10: Strengthen the Mechanics of Your Job Search by Taking the Show on the Road.
Using your marketing resume, special emphasis is given on how to answer ads, work with employment agencies and executive search firms, and network. How to develop a two-minute pitch, how to target recruiters, networking, and using direct-mail strategies to capture the "hidden" job market.

Chapter 11: Key Interview and Salary Issues. Remember your wonderful stories?
Emphasize using Problem–Action–Result (PAR) during the interview. Activities are arranged **before**, **during** and **after** *the interview. A simple but effective interview model is illustrated and reviewed. Final issues: salary strategies, PAR-based long thank-you letters, and invaluable group-interview tactics.*

Chapter 12: Does Age Matter? Age and savvy beats youth and skill every time.
Yes it does—but it is bigger in your mind then the hiring person's. With the marketing resume emphasizing your value and fit before showing age, you are able to tilt the argument in your favor. Techniques are reviewed to minimize age bias while better managing your image. Reviewing the methods for turning age to an advantage. 230

Note: Answers to the quizzes used throughout the book are found at the end of each chapter.

SHORTEN YOUR JOB SEARCH:

Build Confidence, Communicate Your Value and Quickly Land Your New Job

CHAPTER 1

Understand the Hiring Process

It sounds simplistic, but until you have gone through the process of figuring yourself out—your professional and personal goals and your past accomplishments—then you cannot explain yourself to anyone else with conviction, let alone salary potential. If you don't know the product that you're selling, how can you expect a new employer to "buy" or hire you?

"Until one is committed, there is hesitancy and the chance to draw back. Concerning all acts of initiative (and creation), there is one elementary truth…that the moment one definitely commits oneself, then Providence moves too…A whole stream of events issues from the decision, raising in one's favor all manner of unforeseen incidents and meetings and material assistance, which no person could have dreamed would have come his way." William Hutchison Murray, Scottish mountaineer and writer.Let the marketplace, including your current employer, determine if a job is right for you or not. Your job is to maximize interviews at the right level and sell yourself. Whether you want to accept the position comes at the very end of the process, not the beginning.

My strategy is presented from the hiring manager's vantage point, not the Human Resources' view, and is strongly anchored in sales and marketing principles. All hiring executives have two primary concerns when determining whether a candidate fits:

Do you have the technical skills to do the job?
Does your personality mesh with the organization's culture?

And executives assess a candidate's fit by determining:

Have you solved similar problems to the ones they currently have?
Does your resume (and later your interview) communicate how you add value?

A traditional resume that includes your career objective and work history has a very low probability of getting you hired. The chance that your objective matches the hiring executive's is slim. Also, the hiring executive has to search through your resume to identify, interpret and infer your skills and values.

The typical resume presentation of historical title, achievement, and responsibility-based work experience leaves it up to the hiring executive to guess what problems your responsibilities and achievements solved, and what actions you took to solve those problems.

Our strategy and marketing resume uses a fundamentally different paradigm that ensures employers can quickly and accurately assess your fit.

Your technical abilities are clearly spelled out.

Your ability to solve problems similar to the hiring executive's is readily apparent.

Your true work personality is accurately reflected through 360°feedback.

Using our strategy to create a marketing resume gets you:

- noticed and interviewed more often.
- more offers at better compensation.

A Spencer Stuart recruiter, one of America's leading executive search firms (headhunter), in commenting on our marketing resume, said: "I wouldn't change a thing. You made the recruiter's job easier."

In a nutshell, this book will teach you to think like your customer, the hiring executive, and be better able to communicate how you can add **value**.

So bring an open mind, you won't be disappointed.

I will give you a competitive advantage over everyone else in the job market. Since all books position the job seeker from the HR side, those who understand my marketing and sales strategies and apply them to their job-search efforts will achieve a heightened awareness and greater self-confidence, in addition to a competitive advantage. And it is this self-confidence that will greatly assist in advancing your career.

The objective of **SHORTEN YOUR JOB SEARCH** is to help you:

- stand out from the crowd,
- demonstrate your value, and
- show how you will fit in.

The main theme is to strengthen your personal selling skills. This will be achieved by emphasizing:

- the importance of the resume and its role in the hiring process,
- the use of sophisticated direct-mail cover letters, and

- the need to give special attention and effort to the "closing process" during and after the interview.

So, let's get started. We will follow the motto of Peter Diamondis, chairman and CEO of XPrize Foundation and the founder of more than a dozen high-tech companies: "The best way to predict the future is to create it yourself."

"Dear Lloyd,

Writing my own resume was like gazing into a pool of water and not seeing my reflection. With your excellent resume writing technique, however, I now see my skills and abilities as I've never seen them before.

Thank you for your consistent help and support during this emotional project. You're worth a million dollars! Now, as I look into the pool of water, I see a glittering smiling face in return. "
-C.P., Sales Associate, Ritz Bakery & Delicatessen

Hmm, C.P. experienced what Doris Lessing, winner of the Nobel Prize for Literature, said: "That is what learning is. You suddenly understand something you've understood all your life, but in a new way."

CHAPTER 2

Learn the Three Key Factors to Manage Your Career

Hiring executives are buying confidence.

Some years ago, I met with a financial officer for a free initial consultation. At the time he was employed and earning a substantial six-figure salary. After our discussion, he went home to review the components of my counseling program. A week later he returned and signed up. As we were preparing to begin the program, I asked him why he decided to sign up?

His response was an eye-opener. He said there were three reasons and he would present them to me in the order of importance.

He first needed to increase his confidence level. This was a big surprise to me, because I assumed if you're a senior executive making good money, you would be very confident. Yet, this wasn't the case.

Second, he needed to be more focused on his past accomplishments. He felt he did not know the "product" he was selling.

Third, he didn't feel a strong sense of ownership with his resume. He felt it failed to adequately communicate the **value** he could bring to a future employer.

Bottom line: During the job-search process, you're selling confidence. Does your resume communicate your confidence adequately? Does it represent your true **value**?

* * *

Let's begin the counseling process. Understand two basic factors about the job market that affect all situations and exist in any type of job market.

First Factor:

The person who gets hired or promoted is not necessarily the person who is best qualified. Rather, it goes to the person who is *perceived* to be the best qualified. It's not reality that counts; it's perception.

Better managing how you're perceived will give you an important competitive advantage.

Quiz: *(yes/no)*
____ Have you experienced this pattern in hiring?
____ In promotions?
____ In other aspects of your life?

Most clients answered yes to all three questions.

Second Factor:

Job search and trying to move your career forward is a sales issue. You're trying to sell a product: **you**.

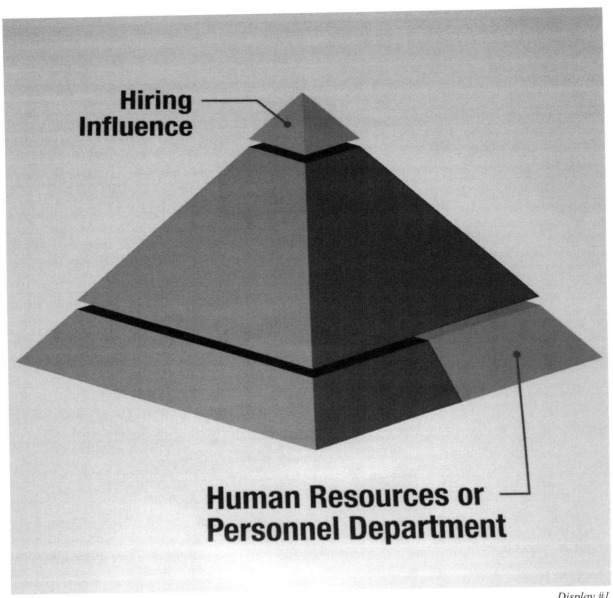

Hiring Influence

Human Resources or Personnel Department

Display #1

Do you agree? *(yes/no)* ___

Most people agree, and since job search is a sales issue, there are three classic issues that must be taken into consideration and acted upon.

1. **It's not what you want to sell, it's what the customer wants to buy**.
   a. Using an objective in your resume violates this concept.
2. **Make it easy for the customer to buy**, and

22

b. People won't take the time to figure out your resume.

3. **Who is your customer**?

    c. In most cases, it's **not** Human Resources.

Superior presentation in your resume can beat out better education and better experience, because improved presentation in your resume can satisfy these three sales issues while the traditional resume format ignores them. These issues will be discussed in greater detail later.

    This book is constructed to teach you **Personal Selling Skills**.

Now we're going to cover the three sales issues in inverse order.

Quiz: Who are the salespeople in your job search, i.e., who will help sell you into a new position?

    ____ yourself
    ____ Human Resources recruiters
    ____ agency recruiters
    ____ hiring executives
    ____ business contacts
    ____ networking contacts
    ____ all of the above

The correct answer is _____.

Which person will make the "buying" decision? _____

If you answered "hiring executives," you're correct. It is, however, worth repeating that your audience during the job search is not the HR department. Though the department does screen resumes for all other departments in its organization, HR only hires for its own department. And remember, it does not screen in, it screens out! Also since all company websites are managed by the HR department, ask yourself: If I'm not interested in working in HR, then why am I sending my materials to the HR department? During your job search, HR is your main gatekeeper or "enemy." Even senior HR executives agree with this view. Their job is to control the organization's hiring process and that usually works against the job candidate.

Why do people send their resume to the Human Resources department? Clients have said:

    ____ I want to work in the HR department.

____ The company website tells you. (Question: What department manages the daily operation of the company's employment website? You guessed it: HR.)

____ The advertisement tells you to respond to HR.

____ I've always sent my materials to HR.

But the "Black Hole" in the hiring process turns out to be the Human Resources department.

Here's the $64 question: How do you get past the HR department to the hiring executive?

Answer: Write directly to the hiring executive, and use a marketing letter *without* your resume. This approach is explained in Chapter 9, Book One, on the use of Direct Mail.

Two of the largest obstacles in landing a new position are age and lack of industry experience. Though these two issues play a part, the major concern from the hiring executive's viewpoint is: Can you solve my problems and make me or save me money? What's in it for me? (WIIFM)

Job-search expert Tom Jackson (*Guerrilla Tactics in the New Job Market*) sums up the universal law of hiring: "Any employer will hire any applicant so long as he or she is convinced that it will bring more value than it costs."

Simple concept but universal. Conclusion: All you have to do to land a new position is demonstrate your **value** *and then communicate it to the hiring person. This book guides you through discovering, defining and articulating your value to prospective employers. All you have to do is stay the course and complete the entire book.*

The solution to your career issues is not more experience or education, but better presentation of your existing work history and accomplishments. You don't need an MBA. You need presentation because you're better than you think you are, and this book will demonstrate that fact.

How well are you at "selling" yourself with your current resume, and how well do you sell yourself during the interview process?

In my experience, job-search anxiety, stress and frustration can be greatly reduced by expanding the knowledge of the product you're selling and of the hiring process. Let me show you how.

The Hiring Model: Learning to Play the Game

Albert Einstein said it best: "You have to learn the rules of the game. And then you have to play better than anyone else."

To identify, interview and land a new position quickly, it is important to understand what information hiring managers and executives want in a successful candidate. This chapter will discuss what that data consist of, and how to get it into your resume.

Let's take an in-depth look at the "sales issue" in the context of job search. But first, a question: Is the crux of the job-search issue a sales problem?

Identify the three basic sales principles:

    a. ____ cross-sell whenever possible
    b. ____ it's not what you're selling, it's what the customer wants to buy
    c. ____ only continuous action counts
    d. ____ resume is a sales presentation
    e. ____ make it easy for the customer to buy
    f. ____ price is only an issue in the absence of value
    g. ____ it's not reality that counts; it's perception

Who's your customer? Which individual will decide to hire you and pay a salary with benefits? Let's review this issue in detail.

An Insider's View of the Job Market and Hiring Process

"True marketing starts out…with the customer, his demographics, his realities, his needs, his values. It does not ask, What do we want to sell? It asks, What does the customer want to buy?"
The Essential Drucker by Peter F. Drucker

"Believe nothing, no matter where you read it or who has said it, not even if I have said it, unless it agrees with your own reason and your own common sense."
Buddha

For people in job transition, the HR department is not the main gatekeeper limiting a candidate's ability to generate interviews and job offers. It's not even the lack of industry experience. Rather, it's the executive recruiter's and the hiring executive's desire for basic information in the first 10 seconds when they review your resume, and secondly, the quality of "sales support" materials during the interview process.

*This book will teach you a better way to communicate your **value** to a prospective or current employer.*

Large Sections of the Working Public Don't Get It! "It's Sales, Stupid!!"

In managing your career, there are two cardinal rules that can't be ignored, because they strongly influence all aspects of career management and the search process.

The person who gets hired or promoted is not the person who is always the best qualified. Rather, it goes to the person who is **perceived** to be the best qualified. In the real world it is not reality that counts; it's perception. Your resume makes the first impression, and if it is not selling you, it's killing you!

Looking for a job or position with a current or new employer is basically a sales issue. Therefore, we know what the solutions are: they're sales solutions—not technical solutions or human-resource solutions, but **sales** solutions.

Certain large categories of employees "get it." They understand that job search is a sales issue. They include people in sales, marketing, promotion, advertising, public relations, corporate communications, etc. Those that don't get it are usually found in technical areas such as engineering, the sciences, information technology, finance, education, and some of the helping professions.

Therefore, from the recruiter's perspective, the resume is seen as a simulation for those who "get it." That is, if you're in the selling professions, your resume should have a strong sales quality and not look like a document from an accounting or information technology professional. This is a subtle point, but critical to job-search success.

Quiz: **Assign the job category into the appropriate column.**

Don't Get It   **Get It**

Corporation Communications

Helping Professions

Sales

Education

Public Relations

Finance

Marketing

Information Technology

Promotion

Sciences

Advertising

Engineering

Crux of the Job-Search Issue

People who have managed a department and had to hire are familiar with the recruiting process. Let's review it in detail. As we do, compare the **hiring model** to your personal work experience. If the model matches, it's highly recommended that you adopt the strategies and techniques described throughout the book.

It is essential to understand that the job-search challenge and much of the career management issue that people face is basically a **sales problem**. So if you normally wear a "technical hat," i.e. your background and experience are in financial, information technology, engineering, chemical, medical and scientific fields, you will need to replace it with a "sales hat." Understand that regardless of your personal situation, to advance your career it is necessary to see yourself as a **product**. Then you need to define yourself as a product and finally market yourself like a product. This process is what our marketing friends call branding, or packaging yourself to be sold.

Implication: If we're in agreement that the root problem in job search is a sales problem, then we know what the solutions should be. They're sales solutions.

As we construct the hiring model, it is important to compare these ideas and concepts to your actual experience. Learn to be critical of the information you receive during your search. Don't accept information and job strategies on face value. Instead, always compare the information to your experience and common sense.

Key Principle: The person who gets hired or promoted is not always the person who is best qualified. Rather, it goes to the person who is perceived to be the best qualified. **It is not reality that counts; it is perception**. Are we in agreement? _____

From this basic truth about the human condition flow three central **selling rules**.

Rule #1: **It's not what you want to sell, rather it's what your customer wants to buy!** This is the first law of sales.

Review your current resume.

Does your resume have an objective? ___Yes ___No

If so, you're violating this rule. Why are you talking about your needs? From the reader's standpoint, your needs don't count in the hiring equation, because it's not about what you want to sell. It's about what the customer (the hiring person) wants to buy.

While counseling an executive secretary, I asked why she had a particular accomplishment on her resume. She replied, because that accomplishment took her to San Francisco … and she loved San Francisco. Again, this illustrates the self-centered thinking of job candidates.

* * *

The difficulty with the objective is that it represents the need of the candidate, not the hiring executive. And in the hiring process, your future employer doesn't care what your needs are. That's not his or her concern. It is yours. Remember that the job-search process is not about you. It's about your client, your audience, or your potential employer. They're interested in the **value** you bring to the party, not your destination.

Rule #2: **Make it easy for the customer to buy.**

This is where most people in job search drop the ball.

In your resume, you must talk about the needs of your hiring audience, and this must be done in an easy and efficient manner. The amount of time you have with the reader of your resume is initially 10 seconds or less. If your resume is in the wrong format, you don't even get 10 seconds. Finally, you must speak the language of business: dollars, percentages and jargon/industry terminology.

Quiz: Qualities in your resume (Answer yes or no)
    ____ Has a personality description?
    ____ Each skill/area of expertise is described in detail?
    ____ Identified the problems you solved?
    ____ Heavy use of numbers or percentages?
    ____ Heavy use of jargon or industry terminology?
    ____ Use dates when you graduated from college?
    ____ Use personal data?
    ____ Use interests?
    ____ Has a specific focus?
    ____ Explained what business your employers were in?
    ____ Used a two- to three-page resume?

If you answered no to most of the above, you're making it difficult for your customers to buy, by failing to provide the necessary information to determine if you can do the job, solve their problems and fit with the company's management team.

Rule #3: **Who are your customers and how do they think?**

Let's take a closer look at your customer during the hiring process. Most people experience frustration during their search. This is true when revising their marketing materials, especially their resume. A lot of this confusion is due to the conflicting advice people receive, both directly from associates and outplacement counselors, and indirectly from books and articles on the topic. In fact, at last count, there are more than 300 books in print on how to construct and write a resume, and even more online. Much of this information adds to the confusion and frustration, because the starting point from which their discussion is written is based on the hiring viewpoint of the Human Resources department, not executives who hire.

Most companies and organizations are constructed like a pyramid, with Human Resources at the bottom and the hiring influence at the top. With the exception of those who want to work in Human Resources, HR is not your customer. The hiring influence is your customer. Employment information coming down the organization from the hiring influence receives a much better reception than those resumes that HR is trying to send up through the organization.

The hiring influence speaks two languages, and it's important that your resume speaks these two languages.

1. Jargon or technical language. By using jargon, you're viewed as an insider rather than a novice. If hired, you can come up to speed quickly, because you require little or no training. From the hiring person's perspective, you can save time and money. Good reason to hire you.
2. Numbers. The person who will hire you is a "numbers person." So speak his or her language.

I've been a member of the Financial Executive Network Group (FENG) for many years and have counseled more than 125 financial executives, including CFOs, vice presidents of finance, treasurers, controllers and assistant controllers. During this time, I've noticed a strange phenomenon. Many financial executives use little or no numbers in their resume. And yet, they are applying for a senior financial position and will report to a senior executive that lives and dies by the numbers. What's going on?

The only explanation that I've come up with is that financial executives, when they transition from the corner office to job search, shift from thinking like a hiring influence to thinking like a job-search candidate. And they present their credentials the way they think the HR department wants the information. Fatal mistake.

Bottom line: This story illustrates the need for job seekers to think like their customers (audience). You have to stop thinking like a candidate, and instead think like the hiring influence and provide the information they require to make an **informed hiring decision**.

* * *

Executives and managers require answers to only three issues to reach their hiring decision.
1. Can you do the job technically? WIIFM (what's in it for me)?
2. Have you solved the same type of problems we are experiencing?
3. Will you fit? Is there good chemistry? Do I like you?

Since most executives and managers think like this, let's try to agree on a common approach to the hiring process. Most people can relate to this premise; do you?

Quiz: Answer true or false
_____1. Your resume is written for a specific, well-defined audience, such as the Human Resources department.
_____2. The language of the person who will hire you is to make or save money, i.e., profit.
_____3. You should put your personality on the resume because managers hire in their own image.
_____4. To focus your reader, begin your resume with an objective.
_____5. You have at least 30 seconds when someone first reviews your resume.
_____6. Your resume should not differentiate yourself from the competition. It is better not to stand out from the crowd.
_____7. Perception is more important on the resume than reality.
_____8. Job search is first and foremost a sales problem.
_____9. In constructing your resume, make it easy for your customers to buy.
_____10. Human Resources is your most important customer.

BASIS OF ALL HIRING

Remember the last time that you had to replace a key member on your staff, one that reported directly to you. Now assume you had to replace an individual because of his or her inability to get the job done. In going through the resume review and the interview process, hiring executives concentrate on **three central issues**:

1. Can the candidate do the job technically?

If not, you're no longer under consideration and your resume is discarded. If you can do the job technically, the next issue is phrased in personal terms. Can you get the "monkeys" or problems off of the hiring executive's back? Think of it in military terms: Rank has its privileges. The hiring executive doesn't want to call those SOBs to collect his receivables. You do it. You do the month-end reconciliation. He earned his stripes, it's now your turn. That's why he hired you.

2. Have you solved our type of issues or problems?

If you can do the job technically, hiring executives phrase this question in selfish terms. If I hire you, can you make me money? Save me money? Help me get a raise or promotion? Can you feed my wallet and bank account? In a phrase: What's In It For Me (WIIFM) if I hire you?

WIIFM is the most powerful radio station on the planet, broadcasting a powerful message. Can you make me money? Save me money? Make me look good? Help me get a raise, promotion or bigger bonus? Can you feed my wallet or bank account?

3. If hired, would the candidate be able to get along with members of my management team?

The hiring influence will always ask the technical question first. If the candidate can't do the job technically, there's no reason to bother asking the other questions. If you can do the job technically and solve the company's problems, you have satisfied two of the three key factors for any hiring manager.

Critical issue? The hiring influence has two basic motivators: Can you do the job technically and solve my problems? And if I hired you, what's in it for me? These two issues are very closely related and can be imagined as two sides of the same coin. In the mind of the hiring influence, however, only one of them always comes first. Which one?

_____ Solve my problems _____ WIIFM

STORY

Let me illustrate the correct answer. Imagine that you and I both work for a major cereal company. You're a district manager and I'm your regional sales manager. The company then launches a new cereal product, and you fail to obtain shelf space in the supermarkets in your territory for this new product. As your RSM, I'll fire you because of your failure to make your numbers, which causes me to fail to make my numbers. In other words, the RSM can't achieve WIIFM unless you *first* solve the *problem* of obtaining shelf space. This shows that most hiring influences are motivated first and foremost by having their problems solved and secondly by self-interest.

***

Paradigm Shift: Your audience in the job search is not results-oriented but **problem**-oriented. This is a shift in most people's outlook on the job-search process. Now look at your resume. Notice that all the accomplishments in your resume are only expressed in action and/or results terminology. That, however, is not the orientation of the hiring audience. They're problem oriented! Your resume accomplishments need to show that you can solve their problems.

In the hiring model, the amount of time your reader will devote to your resume is usually only 10 seconds.

This is what I call your "window of opportunity." Since resume responses to ads and Internet postings often come in the thousands, the reader of your resume and cover letter is presented every day with the same problem. With such high-volume responses, he or she can only give each response a short amount of time—usually 10 seconds. Where should the reader put their time—in the cover letter or in the resume? Since it's not possible to skim a cover letter, the reader will put his or her 10 seconds into skimming your resume.

Take a minute to review your resume. Do you provide the hiring influence with the answers to the three critical hiring questions above? If not, you're making it difficult for your customer to buy. Why?

Insider's tip: Did you know that professional recruiters in the Human Resources department and executive recruiters can skim a resume in only 10 seconds? Here's how they do it. They simply look for three patterns.

1. Are you a job hopper? This can be determined easily by scanning the dates of your employment. Six jobs in two years disqualify you.

2. Is there a progression in title? This is the best reference you can have because it is objective.
3. Is there a progression in salary? The reader of your resume should never get this information from your document. Leave it off.

The implication of how HR reviews a resume is that your document should, if possible, show at least one progress in job title on the first page. And it will be necessary to try to avoid being perceived as a job hopper. How this is accomplished will be discussed later in the book.

Quiz: Answer true or false

___1. Technical ability to do the job is the first milestone to satisfy in constructing your resume.
___2. WIIFM is the most important radio station to listen to during job search.
___3. If you can't do the job technically, you still can get hired for the position.
___4. The hiring influence always asks the technical question at the end of a resume review.
___5. Solving a manager's problems is more important than making or saving money for the company.
___6. Most hiring decisions are based on a candidate's ability to do the job technically, solve the company's problems, and fit in terms of personality.
___7. Hiring managers are selfish and want to know what's in it for them if they hire you.
___8. The initial read of a person's resume is 30 seconds.
___9. Recruiters can evaluate your resume in 10 seconds.

Decision to Hire

Based on my experience as an HR director, participant feedback from 28-plus years of presenting seminars, counseling more than 3,500 clients, and comments from 35-plus senior HR executives, between 80 and 90 percent of the decision to hire is based on chemistry / fit / personality. Do I like you? Do I trust you? Will you get along with the other people in my department? If not, I can't hire you, because I have worked too hard to recruit, train, and get my people to work as a team. I will not put a bad apple in the barrel, regardless of how good you are technically.

Also related to the "Do I like you?" question is the fact that most hiring executives and managers hire in their own image. Jocks hire jocks, ex-military types hire ex-military types, bulls in the china shop will hire other bulls, and easygoing, laissez-faire types will hire other easygoing, laissez-faire types. It all comes down to the fact that people hire in their own image—the human condition factor again. Even so, few resumes attempt to address this critical issue. Our strategy avoids this mistake.

How you build your personality into your resume will be discussed at great length in a later chapter.

Only 10 to 20 percent of the decision to hire is based on technical ability. Can you do the job and solve my problems? Can you get the monkeys off of my back and put them on your back?

The reason the decision is so lopsided is because of the motivation of the hiring manager. He/she simply asks: "What's in it for me?" What do I get out of the hiring decision? Yet, for the great majority of resumes, the technical issue comprises a majority of the content.

Quiz

1. In your job search, who makes the final hiring decision?

__ HR __ Department head __ Recruiter

2. What has more influence over the hiring decision: __ perception or __ reality?

3. Circle the letter below of the three key sales rules in job search.

a. True marketing starts with the customer.

b. Job search is a sales problem.

c. Who is the hiring influence and how do they think?

d. Evaluate against your experience—what you read and hear during job search.

e. It's not what you want to sell; rather, it is what the customer wants to buy.

f. Most books on writing resumes are written from the HR perspective.

g. Make it easy for the customer to buy.

h. Unless you want to work in the personnel department, HR is your "enemy."

Here is a SUMMARY OF THE HIRING MODEL.

- Your audience is the hiring influence or hiring manager, not the HR department.
- The hiring influence has several motivators: Can you do the job and get the monkeys off my back; if I hire you, what's in it for me? Will you fit with my management team?
- The hiring influence sees the resume as a "risk-reduction document."
- The hiring influence is not results-oriented, but problem-oriented.
- The hiring influence speaks two languages: jargon and numbers.
- The amount of time the hiring influence will give to reading your resume is 10 seconds.
- And finally, the hiring influence runs her or his department based on one concept: **No surprises**.

Over the last 28 years, I have presented this model to more than 15,000+ seminar participants in every job category and representing every industry. Everyone agreed that this model is an accurate representation of how people hire. One group, however, disagreed with one aspect of the model. A group of 35 senior human resources executives agreed with this entire model, including that HR was the "enemy." They acknowledged their role as the company gatekeeper.

What they disagreed with was that the decision to hire was not 80 percent chemistry and 20 percent ability to do the job. They said it was 90 percent chemistry and only 10 percent ability to do the job! And **most people use a resume format that ignores 90 percent of the hiring decision**. It's not surprising, therefore, that job searches are taking longer than necessary, and people are failing to achieve a "good fit" with their new employer. If 90 percent of the hiring decision is ignored when constructing the resume, why should people expect quick results in their job search? How to build chemistry, personality and fit into the resume will be covered in a later chapter.

Answers to Quizzes:

- *Who are the sales people in your job search?—all of the above.

- *Identify the three basic sales principles—"b, e, and g"

- *Assign the job category into the appropriate column.

Don't Get It	Get It
Helping Professions	Corporate Communications
Education	Sales
Finance	Public Relations
Information Technology	Marketing
Sciences	Promotion
Engineering	Advertising

- *Common Approach to the Hiring Process
1. F, 2. T, 3. T, 4. F, 5. F, 6. F, 7. T, 8. T, 9. T, 10. F

- *For hiring influence, what always comes first?—solve my problems

- Answer true or false

1.T, 2. F, 3. F, 4. F, 5.T, 6.T, 7.T, 8. F, 9.T

- *Quiz
1. Department head
2. Perception
3. b, e, g

CHAPTER 3

CAREER PLANNING: WHAT NEXT?

You got the job, have been there awhile; comfortable? Finished, right? No! Why Not?

STORY

At a local self-help group, I met a young industrial design engineer who expressed a desire to make a radical career change. During our initial counseling meeting, I asked why he had decided to become an engineer. He responded that his two brothers and his father were all engineers and in high school, both math and science came easily to him. So he went to a premier engineering university and graduated with a B.S. degree in industrial engineering.

I asked him when it was that he realized he didn't like engineering. He replied that it was during his sophomore year. Did he consider changing majors? "No," he said. "I am not a quitter." Upon graduation, he was recruited by a prestigious medical-supply corporation to design surgical needles. But after only 18 months on the job, he concluded he strongly disliked the work. So to improve his chances of moving elsewhere in the corporation, he decided to get a master's degree in, you guessed it, design engineering. After only one year of part-time graduate study, he realized he disliked the graduate study program. When I asked him if he considered changing majors, he again said "No, I'm not a quitter."

He finished the degree and received a promotion at work. After 10 years, however, his frustration with work finally culminated with his resignation and decision to become a social worker. He finally realized that to achieve job satisfaction, he had to learn to be a "quitter." Then we were able to work successfully to achieve his goal.

* * *

Most of us during our careers have questioned why we hold on to the type of job we have. A recent news survey found that more than 70 percent of the workforce would rather be doing something else to make a living. In this chapter, the issue of "What next?" in our careers will be reviewed in detail.

The best place to start is to validate your present employment situation. If out of work, the answer is easy. You need to look for a new position. If you're employed, it's a more difficult decision: Should you stay or leave your job? Let's tackle these tough issues now so you can better manage your career long-term.

* * *

Stay or Leave?

"There is yet time enough for you to take a different path."
Chinese fortune cookie

Many signs tell you when to begin looking for a new position. Don't let "golden handcuffs" prevent you from making a job change that could advance your career and greatly increase your job satisfaction.

If for some time you've had the nagging feeling that your work life could be better, rethink your job situation and begin using the concepts and techniques in this book.

Reading the Handwriting on the Wall

When You *Should* Stay In Your Job (even though you're thinking about leaving)

1. When your work has gotten broader in scope and your responsibility has increased, even if your title hasn't changed. But don't stay too long.

2. If your annual raises are at least 4 percent of your salary.

3. When you feel that at one or more key senior persons is watching your career track.

4. When you feel comfortable with the corporate culture and you can see yourself rising to the level you're after. (It doesn't have to be senior management. Not everyone wants to work 75 hours a week.)

5. When you are learning a great deal from your present job.

6. When you are contributing more than you're learning, but are being paid handsomely in return. One rule of thumb for most fields: Up to 30, you should be making 1.5 to 2.0 times your age in salary. After that, if you're on the way to the top, your salary should jump in leaps and bounds.

7. When the company is actively grooming women, minorities and older employees for senior management or at least makes it known—through memos, recruitment and general approach—that the top spots are not closed to these categories of employees.

When You *Should* Change Jobs (or at least begin to think about it)

1. Effects of mergers, takeovers and restructurings. Employees are most at risk when working for a new boss, or when they must re-earn their stripes. At management levels, it's not so much a matter of competence as chemistry.

2. "Things just aren't working out." Usually the following: a. Incompatible personalities that lead to antagonisms between subordinates and bosses. b. Conflicts over strategy, specifically the direction in which the business should go and how to get there. c. Philosophical differences over management style or ethical issues. d. Disagreement over the subordinate's role within the division.

3. When someone at your level is promoted over you. Find out what's wrong. This may be an indicator that you're viewed as second-rate, true or not.

4. When you're left out of the key decision-making process after previously having participated in that process.

5. When you work long hours but find that only the volume of your work—not the responsibility—has increased in the last six to 10 months.

40

6. If no one (women, minority or older person) has made it to senior management or a partnership at your firm. Unless you expect it to happen to you, and soon, it's probably not going to happen for a long time. Before committing to another job, however, discuss the situation with your bosses if you can.

7. When everything is coming too easily and promotions fall into your lap surprisingly quickly. You might be set up for a fall later on. Perhaps the company only needs a female or minority in a certain spot, and is ignoring your developmental needs. Recognize your growth requirements and make sure you get the required training.

8. If you've been in the same job for years and are bored.

9. When you're working for a slow-moving superior.

10. When—after checking the marketplace—you realize you are underpaid.

11. You have that nagging gut feeling that your work life could be better, or you feel trapped. If you checked off two or more items, give serious consideration to changing jobs.

Remember: As hard as it may seem, don't take a potential job loss personally. Remind yourself that it's a business deal. You can be quite sure that's how your boss sees it. Also, many clients have used the techniques in this program to advance their careers with their current employer. Whether you seek a position with a new employer or advance at your current one, the process is basically the same.

Deciding to Take a Job Where You May Fail

STORY

After four years as director of training for Bellevue Medical Center in New York City, I left non-profit employment and joined a small $130 million company in West Caldwell, N.J., called Cadence Industries Corporation. They owned the Marvel Entertainment Group (comics/licensing), Hudson Vitamin, Curtis Circulation, and several smaller companies. I joined Cadence as the corporate training manager reporting to the director of human resources.

From the beginning, I was heavily engaged in preparing and presenting basic supervisory training programs to executives and managers throughout the corporations' many business units. The initial program was on behavioral interviewing skills for managers. After eight months, one Friday afternoon, I was called to the office of the chief financial officer, who informed me that my boss had been terminated. The CFO then explained that, based on my performance and the visibility I had gained with my training programs, the company was prepared to offer me my former boss's position on a 90-day probationary basis. If successful, the title and raise would be applied retroactively to next Monday's date. The CFO requested that I think about the offer over the weekend, review it with my wife, and then meet with him on Monday. It was pointed out that if I accepted the challenge and failed to perform satisfactorily, I could remain the training manager. If successful, I could hire a replacement training manager.

To say the least, I went home with this 800-pound gorilla on my shoulders. I could hardly sleep. I kept turning the job offer over in my mind. The basic facts were:

1. I had been working at the company for only eight months.

2. The only supervisory experience I had was as an absentee supervisor for the benefits manager at Bellevue for one year.

3. My main expertise was training and development. I had no actual experience in recruiting, even though I was teaching the topic, and my seminar participants were using the model I presented with great success. In addition, I had no experience with other responsibilities in the human resources function, including wage and salary administration, policies and procedures, benefits, and most importantly, recruiting.

4. My 13-year career up to that time was mainly training and development. As a result, I concluded I would be over my head if the position were accepted. Nevertheless, I kept rethinking the offer. I knew that I wanted to accept the opportunity but had great hesitation. Could I do the job? What if I failed? Would I be at a dead-end in the position? After much soul searching, I came to one basic conclusion. I did not really know the responsibilities of the director of human resources. But the CFO to whom the position reported did. And if he, representing the company, thought I could do the job, then I could do the job. The following Monday, I met with the CFO and accepted the position. It was the beginning of a successful four-year career with the corporation.

* * *

Try this little exercise: Ask yourself, who is best capable of evaluating your father as a husband? It's not the children, or any relatives, and most importantly, it is not your father. Only your mother is capable. Likewise, in considering a particular position, the person who is best qualified to evaluate you for that position is the person to whom the position reports. It's not you. So grab that brass ring. *You are better than you think you are.*

* * *

Finding a Good Place to Work

The evaluation summary below, though not directly related to the above two issues, can help you better define the qualities you're looking for in a next position, whether with a current or future employer.

Even if your analysis confirms that you should stay in your current position, to maximize future career opportunities with your present employer, it is advantageous to have an updated marketing resume that can provide ammunition for your next performance review or job posting.

1. Don't go to a firm to change things overnight. • Go to a firm that does mediocre work (i.e., expects only average work performance) and, slow but surely, in self-defense, you'll be doing mediocre work. • Instead, go where you've got everything going for you already— then make your contribution by doing your best.

2. Don't spend too much time deciding between big firms and small firms. • More critical than the size of a firm is the size of the firm's people. • There are big people in business and there are small people, and you'll find them at every size company. • The little people will never stop trying to impress you with their contributions. The big people will allow you to make your own.

3. Refuse to work for anyone who isn't better than you are. • While your boss might not be better than you are, he probably thinks he is. As a result, you'll be totally frustrated in a wasteland of ordinary work assignments. • It's much better to work for someone you can learn from, whose opinions you respect and who can contribute to making you a better performer than you thought you could be.

4. Find a facilitating environment. • Find yourself someone who evaluates your work without judging you, who can accept your problems as real without putting you down as a person, and who is willing to help you come to your own solutions.

5. Resist the job that's offered because you're good at the wrong things. • Know your areas of expertise, what you're good at and enjoy doing. • Avoid jobs that play on your weaknesses. All buildings must have a secure foundation. So must your career, you build on those strengths of yours that relate most closely to your job.

6. Don't let yourself be wooed into a dumb job. • Ask yourself if it's a job you'd seek out on your own if it wasn't sprung on you. • Remember how quickly a love affair can turn into a cheap romance. • Plan your own career, and know your own objectives. Know where you want to go and how to get there, before the phone rings.

7. The sorriest "people" are those who are overqualified. • All I wanted to do was get out of a bad situation. So I accepted a job that had no need for my special abilities and skills. • This situation leads to fill-in-the-blank assignments and being sent as a warm body to do dull work. • Stay where you are, no matter how unhappy, until someone is ready to appreciate you for your full value.

8. Remember that this business has to be fun. • If the job looks like honest work but not honest fun—nothing to learn and no creative challenge—then avoid it.

9. Listen to the three most reliable sources of advice. • Talk to people who already work there. Ask about the things you consider critical. Does the company live up to its promises? Is your work area critical to the company or is it merely the factory? How are the little people treated? • Ask someone who just quit why he or she did so. • Listen to that wee small voice in the back of your own head during the interview. Trust your feelings. "Dive deep into the data, then trust your gut."— Andy Grove, former chairman of Intel

Bottom line: Betray any one of these nine points and you'll betray yourself at the same time and be looking for another job within a short time.

* * *

What do you want to do next in your career?

Chinese proverb: If you don't know where you're going, any road will get you there!

Buddha quote: "Believe nothing, no matter where you read it or who has said it, unless it agrees with your own reason and your own common sense."

What do you want to do when you grow up?

Though many people think they want a career change, from industrial designer to social worker, few people really want such a radical move. Rather, most want to advance their career by getting promoted, transferring to another area, or joining an organization where their expertise and experience are recognized, competitively compensated, and challenged— and where they have the opportunity for personal and professional growth.

In my many years as a career counselor, I have encountered only six people who genuinely wanted to make a radical career change.

For those genuine career changers, I would recommend the book *Do What You Are: Discover the Perfect Career for You Through the Secrets of Personality Type*, by Paul Tieger and Barbara Baron-Tieger. A quicker assessment, however, can be found in two articles by T. Butler & J. Waldroop: "Is Your Job Your Calling?" (*Fast Company*) and "Finding the Job You *Should* Want" (*Fortune*).

The second article contains a short version of the authors' long career inventory. I have employed the inventory with more than 50 clients and also presented the inventory in self-help groups to more than 300 participants. They generally agreed that the inventory was quite accurate. In fact, I took the inventory myself three times over a two-year period, and each time it confirmed that I was in the position that best fit my interests and skills. So give it a try. Most people have found that the results of the inventory confirm that they are in the type of job that matches their interest.

45

For the great majority of people who want to make a job change, this book will be their ticket to success, because most people want to make a job change to a position that offers stability, challenge, growth, and an opportunity to make a meaningful contribution, along with fair compensation.

Most people, when they lose a job, immediately update their resume. Wrong! Wrong! Wrong! Now all they have is an updated, bad document. The first step must be self-assessment: define the product you're selling and define what your customer wants to buy, then match the two together. Isn't this what marketing is all about? Isn't marketing the basis of all successful sales?

Also, think for a minute about where confidence comes from. It doesn't come from looking in the mirror and telling yourself how great you are. No, it comes from self-knowledge. You need to know your accomplishments, which problems you've solved, what you're most proud of, the dollars you made or saved for your employers. This can only be accomplished through the comprehensive self-assessment covered in Chapter 5.

The other critical component will be your ability to communicate your accomplishments to others so they are able to become your "salespersons." Self-knowledge is of little value if you can't communicate it easily to others, especially during the job-search process and the performance review process.

The noted British management consultant, Gary Hamel, an expert on strategy, said: "There can be no innovation in the creation of strategy without a change in perspective." The objective of my two books has been to change your perspective on the job-search process.

Issues to Consider

It is very difficult to go through the job-search process alone because **you need feedback and validation** during the process.

Thoughts on making a career change

1. By going into a new career, you will most probably be considered "the new kid on the block," and only command a low starting salary.

2. Financial advisors to high-net-worth clients take a minimum of two years to begin building a serious client base. During that time, they earn between $13,000 and $18,000, even if they are sponsored by a large financial service company like American Express.

3. When considering insurance sales, industry statistics show turnover for new sales representatives at 300 percent the first year; thus, the entire new-hire workforce leaves the job after selling to all their relatives, and after only four months.

4. "You must use theory as a basis for action. Theory without action is useless. Action without theory is very costly."— W. Edwards Deming, American statistician.

5. If a person wanted to make a career of sales, he would have done it in the early years of his career. A financial personality is very different from a sales personality. Past is prologue.

Avoid Inflexibility: What Do I Want to Be When I Grow Up?

A common misconception is that you need a grand plan for your career. We can hardly plan for next week's weather, let alone the variables over a lifetime career. You don't need to know exactly what the perfect next step is in your career. That's not your job either. Rather, let the marketplace and interviewing process demonstrate whether a job is right for you or not. **Your job is to maximize interviews at the proper level and sell yourself.** Whether you want to accept the position comes at the very end of the process, not at the beginning.

* * *

Hanging out your shingle: Going into business for yourself

Over the past 10 years of counseling staff, middle, and senior-level executives, prospective clients frequently express an interest in giving up the "rat race" to go into their own business. Having made this difficult transition in 1984 when I left Oppenheimer & Co., the New York City-based regional brokerage firm, I felt it would be helpful to share the lessons learned and the obstacles faced.

I first had to take a hard look at myself. Who am I? What is my skill set? Who would be interested in what I had to offer? How do I advertise my services? How do I price my services? The questions were many and the answers were few. Ultimately, I learned through the school of hard knocks.

Since I had spent most of my 19-year business career in human resources administration as well as training and development, I naturally decided to become a training consultant to corporations throughout the New York City metropolitan region. I made this decision despite the fact that my book on career changing had been published in 1982. Mentally, I still saw myself as a trainer, not a career coach or advisor.

After two months of working the phones and making numerous sales calls, a number of patterns became obvious. The process was more difficult than I had imagined. The length of time to make the sale became prohibitive. And the buying decision within the company was diffused, as training was sometimes purchased within the HR department, sometimes in sales or even other line departments.

Needless to say, I generated no training assignments. So I began to work my business network for other alternatives. After all, I had bills to pay and a family to support. Through the same business associate that had introduced me to my co-author, Linda Kline, I was able to secure an 18-month, half-time training project with M&M/Mars in Hackettstown, N.J.

With my basic financial needs covered and only half of my work days involved in the training program, I now began to promote my second alternative: building a career counseling and advisory business.

It was at this point that I was introduced to an Italian economist by the name of Pareto who is best known for his principle: the 80/20 rule. Let me explain.

Image a tubular, horizontal object such as a pipe. Entering the left end would be your promotional efforts; exiting from the right end would be the results of those efforts—hopefully sales leads that wind up as sales. In going into business, you must ask yourself a **fundamental question**: What is the main reason you want to start your own business? Is it to promote a service/product or to deliver a service/product? Most managers and executives that I have encountered say that their objective in starting their own business was a desire to deliver some type of service. And often the plan involved a partner. This complicates matters. Often a problem would arise when both partners wanted to devote their time to the deliverables and less or none at all to promotion. Yet, the Pareto principle states that 80 percent of your efforts in building a new business **must be dedicated to promotion**.

In starting a new business, you really only have four choices:

1. Perform both the promotion and delivery of the service yourself. For this to be successful, you should prefer the promotion side versus the delivery side. This is the approach I took when building my counseling practice. Though I consider myself very good at delivery, I get the most personal satisfaction from promoting via talks and seminars. That's where most of my leads come from.

2. Get a partner who prefers promotion. This will allow you to concentrate on the delivery side of the business.

3. Outsource the promotion side while you and your partners concentrate on the delivery.

4. *Don't go into business for yourself.* This last point is critical. Recognize your limitations and don't kid yourself. Remember, most new businesses fail within 18 months because they run out of cash. And this usually happens because the principals are concentrating on delivery instead of promotion.

That's it. There are no other alternatives. Before investing a lot of money, time and emotion into starting your own business that might not survive, make sure you have the promotion issue solved. Building a business is all about promotion, not delivery of your service.

Final point: In the years that I''ve been in the career-counseling business, I have never met a person who was even moderately successful in buying a franchise business and making a go of it. Stay away; you will lose your shirt.

Book recommendation: *Private Consulting* by Barbara Johnson (1982).

* * *

Self-Assessment: Key to Your Future Advancement

Before you rush into the job search, it is vital you know the product you're selling and where you wish to apply your knowledge. Yet, most people jump the gun and begin the search by reaching out to their best networking contacts. Without knowing the product you're selling and its value (self-assessment), it is hard to communicate your value. And it is doubly hard, if not impossible, for your networking contacts to sell you.

Finally: Why Job Search Is Frustrating!

Regardless of your status or job title, most people find the process of looking for a new position to be distasteful and frustrating. Most people hate to look for a new job, for several specific reasons.

Perhaps the biggest is the sheer amount of conflicting advice you receive from various sources. Everyone has a particular opinion on how a resume should be constructed. And it usually reflects the format they used to obtain their current position. Some people will use a functional format, some the combination resume—first page functional and second page chronological—and others will use the inverse chronological resume format. Each case presents numerous variations. What is lacking in all resume formats is a conceptual framework for laying out the information on your work history. Hence, the amount of conflicting or just plain bad advice is massive and is found everywhere—from outplacement counselors, to the more than 300 books in print on resume writing, to newspaper and magazine articles, and from friends, co-workers or acquaintances.

Information Can Relieve Stress

"There is great solace in the simple fact of *clarity*—about what is vital, and what is not."
Good to Great, by Jim Collins, p. 205

Seek accurate information in the face of a stressful situation. If you are worried about a job layoff and uncertainty at work, arm yourself with information about the job market and opportunities elsewhere.

Conflicting and bad information exists at every stage of the job-search process. So how should you evaluate the information you hear or read during your period of transition?

The answer is simple. Compare the information to your background and experience. If it is consistent with your experience, accept it and try to act on it. If the information is contrary to your experience, question it and be skeptical. Ask others for verification.

Many ideas, concepts and strategies in this book are unconventional and may initially sound off the wall. For example, when I discuss the interview, I argued that after the interview, you should write a long thank-you letter, anywhere from two to seven pages, depending on the length of the meeting. Before you reject this strategy, try and understand my logic. If it makes sense to you and fits into your experience, I would hope that you would adopt the strategy of using long thank-you letters.

A second source of frustration stems from the capriciousness of the hiring authorities and gatekeepers—human resources, assistants to hiring executives and managers, agency recruiters and headhunters (search firms), and the hiring influences themselves. In most cases, when these individuals review your resume, they are both judge and jury. And too frequently they provide you with little or no feedback.

A third and perhaps the most serious form of frustration stems from the human resources department. Due to the complexity of the past and current business compliance environment, the HR department cannot allow line managers to control their department's hiring process. The process must be centrally controlled and monitored to prevent illegal hiring techniques and future lawsuits. Company web sites and the resume review process are centralized and controlled by the HR department. Yet, most people fail to realize that HR is their "enemy" during the job search because HR only hires for their own department. They do, however, screen resumes—but not "in." Their main role is to screen *out*.

Once you understand HR's hiring orientation, you must then ask the question, "Why do people send their resumes and cover letters to HR?" The simple answer is that they either don't know better or they're lazy. The solution to this situation is to try to avoid the HR department. An exception to this would be the case where a person wanted to work in HR.

The fourth reason for job-search frustration is that most people fail to distinguish or differentiate themselves from their competition. It is almost impossible to draw the attention of recruiters or hiring executives if your marketing presentations, especially your resume, look like everyone else's. Next time you have the opportunity to review numerous resumes—at a self-help workshop, networking group, or at the outplacement office—do a simple analysis of other people's resumes. What you will discover is what recruiters and headhunters already know: all resumes are constructed in a similar fashion and therefore all look alike. You will now have a better understanding why your job search has failed to achieve the desired results.

If you try to avoid this problem by using a functional or combination resume format, your resume will automatically be discarded. The assumption by the reader of your resume is that you're trying to hide something. And in most cases you are. So stick with the inverse chronological model. It is the only format that is universally accepted. How to construct the resume so that you are viewed as different forms the core issue of my two books. This strategy is not easy, but the steps are simple:

1. Work smarter—what these books are all about, especially how to better communicate your value, and

2. Work harder—apply strategies, methods and techniques that are proven, generate powerful results, and are covered in detail throughout the books.

The real struggle for most people will not be learning what these books teach you. Rather it's forgetting all the bad information and habits of the past.

A major objective of these books is to sharpen your focus, get you to think like your customer, and maximize the number of interviews and offers you can obtain.

Self-Knowledge: Key to Career Success

Before you rush into the job search, it is vital that you know the product you're selling and where you wish to apply your knowledge.

Consider these words of wisdom:

"Luck is preparation meeting opportunity!"—Vince Lombardi (former football coach for the Green Bay Packers)

"I am a great believer in luck, and the harder I work, the more I have of it."
—Thomas Jefferson

"The more you prepare, the less pressure you feel."
—Lawrence Frank, former New Jersey Nets coach

"In the fields of observation chance favors only the prepared mind." – Louis Pasteur

"You can't predict. You can prepare!" —Anonymous

Final Thought: In most cases, what you don't need is more education or certification. What you do need is **presentation**—and that is what these books are all about.

CHAPTER 4

THE BEST WAY TO WIN THE BEST JOB

Know who you are, what you've done, what you can do next. How to be the best in interviews.

STORY

Let's suppose that we own the Ice Capades and have an opening for a skater in one of our traveling shows. Why don't we hire an ex-hockey player? They are some of the finest skaters in the world.

The reason is practical. They don't know the process, which is dance. So we hire a dancer and spend two to three weeks teaching the dancer to skate. If we did it the opposite way by hiring the skater and trying to teach him to dance, it would take forever. Think about someone in your family who is a bad listener. If you sent that person to a training program on listening skills, how long would it take to make them a good listener? How about never?

* * *

The Foundation

All hiring executives have two primary concerns when evaluating a candidate.

- Do you have the technical skill to do the job?
- Does your personality mesh with the organization's culture?

The hiring executive will evaluate a candidate's fit by determining:

- Have you experienced and solved similar problems to the ones they currently face?

- Does your resume (and later your interview) communicate your value?

The marketing resume uses a **fundamentally different paradigm** that ensures employers can quickly and accurately assess your fit.

- Your technical abilities are clear.
- Your ability to solve problems similar to the hiring executive's is readily apparent.
- Your true work personality is accurately reflected.

Using a marketing resume gets you:

- Noticed and interviewed more often.
- More offers at better compensation to choose from.

So how to communicate your **value**?

You don't have to be reminded about the size and quality of the competition you face when applying for a new position. In most industries, the quantity and quality of the applicants has never been greater and of such excellent quality. Add to this the volume of foreign-born talent coming from Asia and you can understand why it is taking so long to land a new job. The issue then is how to compete more successfully?

First Strategy

One interesting aspect of the job market is that it allows people to compete in only two different ways. And ironically most people select the wrong way to compete. You can compete as the best technical person for the job, or compete as the best businessperson for the job. Of the two, which do you think is the best way to compete: technical or business?

Technical vs. Business
Content vs. Process

You're right if you said business-process terms. The problem with trying to compete technically is that someone always has better technical skills.

By coincidence, the hiring manager doesn't want you to compete in technical terms anyway. He or she already has enough "professionals" on his/her staff. This attitude on the part of management was evident in the response one of my clients received from a former boss. He wrote:

> "I agree with the areas of expertise listed. John is a Ph.D. chemist, and like many other Ph.D. chemists, he is going to have a list of technical tools he can utilize or can learn to develop new tools or methods. To me that does not differentiate one Ph.D. from another. The Ph.D. who understands my company's goals and can clearlycommunicate technical options at all levels is what sets that Ph.D. apart."

The Ice Capades story at the beginning of this chapter highlights a very important business concept: *always try to hire process candidates, avoid content candidates* because it is cheaper and more efficient. In the sales context, you hire the good listener and teach them your product line rather than hiring someone who knows your product line but is not a good listener. Regardless of how much time or money a company is willing to spend, you can never teach someone to be a good listener.

Besides, there is the right way, the wrong way, the Army way and our way. So in the end, a company is going to teach their way to do things. Hence, all managers know that you hire based on a candidate's understanding of the business process, not technical knowledge. Yet, most people, especially those with a technical background (information technology, financial, chemical, scientific and engineering) position themselves at a disadvantage by competing technically. Therefore, by shifting your resume's orientation to a strong business orientation, you can gain a distinct competitive advantage in your job search.

"It is best summed up by the mantra from the Harvard education expert Tony Wagner that the world doesn't care anymore what you know; all it cares 'is what you can do with what you know.' " (Source: "How to Get a Job," by Thomas L. Friedman, *New York Times*, May 28, 2013)

So how best to compete?

To successfully compete in this tough job market, use **presentation**, not additional education or certification. Prepare a resume that satisfies the need of employment agencies, executive recruiters and hiring executives. Your competition is following the human resources model, not our hiring model.

Interestingly enough, most business issues or problems are basically the same regardless of industry.

"Most business issues were generic issues—repetitions of familiar problems cloaked in the guise of uniqueness." Source: Roger Lowenstein's review of Peter Drucker's book *The Effective Executive*, *New York Times*, January 22, 2006.

You probably experienced this truth. When you last changed jobs and went to work for a new employer, the business issues you became involved in were basically similar to those you handled at your previous employer. Thus, in presenting your experience in a resume or during an interview, it is important to concentrate on **execution of the basics**. Don't talk about issues of which you were particularly proud. Rather, talk about the issues that the interviewer is concerned about, the monkeys or issues on the hiring executive's back. *Because **the only issue in the job market is the hiring executive's problems**.*

Second Strategy

The second strategy relates to **communicating your value**!

The best way to compete is by telling a complete story when you're communicating your accomplishments. Most people only talk about the **action** they did, and perhaps the **results** they achieved. There is a better way.

Introduction to PAR

PAR stands for:

Problem–Action–Result

PAR is a storytelling method to better communicate the value you can bring to an organization. Other acronyms to describe this approach include SAR (Situation–Action–Result) and CAR (Circumstance–Action–Result). What sets PAR apart from these other forms is our definition for each term.

P = Problem: Universal / generic

When you write about an accomplishment, first identify the issue you're dealing with, and express it in universal business terms. The generic nature of the issue will ensure its widest possible reception. You must, however, talk about issues that resonate with your reader; otherwise, the issue you're discussing will be ignored.

A=Action: Tell *what* you did to solve the issue, *not how*!

If you tell the reader how you solved the problems in your accomplishments they don't need to hire you. You gave it all away for free. My rule is simple: No free consulting. Instead, tell *what* you did, not how you did it.

R=Result: Use $, %, time or testimonials

If possible, quantify your results using dollars made or saved. If dollar figures are unavailable, use percentages or time saved. You can also use a testimonial. For example, how good was the report? It was good enough to go to the board of directors.

It is very important to pay attention to these definitions when constructing your accomplishments in PAR format.

Let me show you an example that illustrates the power of combining these two strategies: shifting from technical content to business process, and using the PAR methodology.

The Power of PAR

This accomplishment was contained in the resume of a digital engineer from the aerospace industry. Like most people, it describes the person's technical competence. It was written by the client as it appeared on his resume. This technical approach kept him out of work for more than 16 months and restricted him to his current industry, aerospace, which was almost nonexistent in New Jersey with only two firms, one of which recently laid him off.

Before:

- Designed and developed 5-channel flight-control system for the Canadair CL-227 "Flying Peanut." The Controller powered three electro-mechanical actuators, two magnetic clutches. The system was controlled by a serial data bus in communication with the autopilot.

This accomplishment is indicative of his entire resume that failed to land employment for 16 months.

After:

For the above accomplishment, we applied the PAR concept and shifted the emphasis from technical competence to business process. The result was powerful.

- To lower manufacturing costs, conceived, designed and built a prototype fin controller which incorporated the elimination of all discrete wiring, use of built-in test software and circuit simplification. Repackaged PC boards. **Result**: Labor dropped from 43 to 16 hours saving $29,000 on initial order, lowered parts count 46% and improved reliability.

This is the rewrite of the above accomplishment written together with the client in the PAR format. This business approach resulted in a new position outside the aerospace industry in less than three weeks and without relocation!

* * *

STORY

A few years ago, I was counseling an executive who obtained an important interview with Marriott International. After discussing the interview with this client, two factors became very clear: First, though the interview lasted one and a half hours, the senior executive who interviewed him had no idea how to conduct a professional interview, and secondly, she took no notes.

Think about this for a moment. This is one of the secret truths of the job market. Those in the job market are often faced with this situation—and if it happens to you (again), you need to be prepared for its ramifications: The higher up the pyramid you interview, the less interviewing ability the executive interviewing you often possesses. They don't know the right questions to ask, leaving you with the desperate need to proactively and effectively communicate your value and how you might "fit" into the organization. And as previously mentioned, making matters worse, this breed of interviewer usually takes few or no notes during the discussion.

When you leave the interview, what does the interviewer remember? What is remembered after one day? Three days? Upon what will they base their decision to bring you back for another interview? Since impressions don't last long, especially if they interview other candidates after you, the only thing left is your resume.

Therefore, the resume, and the process you use to create it, is the single most critical element in a timely and successful job search.

The message in your resume must be clear: It doesn't cost you to hire me, it pays; I bring **value**. If this message is not clearly communicated to the reader, it's time to stop your job search and take a hard look at your resume. Perhaps this is why Financial Executives International distributes a card with a quote, purportedly from George Bernard Shaw. It reads: "The greatest problem with communication … is the illusion that it has been accomplished."

It is very costly to base your job search on illusion.

Most resumes fail to adequately sell prospective employers for several reasons.

First, your expertise is in your chosen field. You're not trained in the job search and self-promotion areas. A long time ago, a Walt Kelly comic strip character named Pogo said it best: "We have met the enemy and he is us." An even *longer* time ago, Abraham Lincoln put it a bit more bluntly: "The attorney who tries his own case has a fool for a client." It is tough seeing the forest for the trees. Still another way to consider the same issue comes from Phil Simms, the former quarterback of the New York Giants. As quoted by a Newark (N.J.) *Star-Ledger* reporter: "(Phil) Simms knew that system (old coach's) as well as anyone. And he admits to having his share of problems learning (Dan) Reeve's (new) scheme. 'It was terrible at first,' he said. 'It's not so much learning the new offense, it's forgetting the old one. That was by far the hardest thing.'"

A marketing client summed it up nicely: "I can market anything except, it seems, myself." He was too close to his career to differentiate clearly between what sells to a prospective employer and what was personally meaningful.

Look at your resume. A lot of accomplishments are there for the wrong reason. Your resume won't sell you by highlighting the aspects of your work history that are important to you—unless they're also important to the hiring executive. Most important to them: Can this person solve the problems our company is facing? Can he or she fit with the rest of my staff?

If you or your resume can't answer those questions, it will greatly limit your job-search success. And to answer those questions, you need to have a clear understanding of what it is that you bring to the table, i.e., your **value**. It's not just a question of getting the interview, it's a question of closing the sale. Since an interview is nothing more than a sales call, most people won't get the job offer if they don't know the product they're selling. In counseling people at all levels for the past 28 years, I've found that everyone comes to the counseling process with **two basic problems**: They don't know the product they're selling, and they don't know what they want to do with the rest of their career. Time for some self-discovery, folks.

Creating a resume that sells is impossible without self-assessment. Without it, you can't talk about your background and experience with authority. You can't violate Vince Lombardi's definition of luck: **preparation meeting opportunity**. Experience has shown that opportunities are of little value without the proper preparation. Ask: do you really know the product you're selling? If not, you're not prepared to do anything but waste those opportunities.

Take some time to reflect on your career. In each position, what was it that you did? What issues did you face? What problems did you solve? What was your *value*? This isn't easy. It's hard to be sure, if you haven't drilled down to the core issues, the basic problems. But it simply must be done if you want to speak the hiring manager's language.

Taking a bad resume and bringing it up to date only creates a bad, up-to-date resume. Without self-assessment—what marketing people call "product knowledge"—many candidates will get the interview but fail to close the sale. Let me illustrate. While giving a presentation to the New Jersey Chapter of Financial Executives International, I opened my presentation by asking the group two questions: 1) Do you honestly feel, if you can get the interview with the hiring executive, that you would be able to close the sale? Get the job offer? Everyone raised his or her hand in agreement. And 2) How many (by a second show of hands) were getting interviews but not getting job offers? Again, everyone's hands went up. It's those trees again—messing up the view of the forest.

Finally, in the *New York Times* business section , the Executive Life column ran an article entitled: "Disguising the Signs of Being 'Outplaced.' " Let me give you a few quotes from this article. "I get outplacement resumes by the dozen—and you can always tell. They all look so artificial, with the same kind of paper and the same kind of 'mission statements.'" "The extent an individual looks like the prepackaged product of outplacement—bland and utterly generic—the job seeker is doing him or herself a great disservice," said John Lucht, an executive recruiter. "There's no question a standardized look hurts a job seeker's chances," said Thomas J. Flynn of a Norwalk, Conn.-based market research firm.

In summary, start with **self-assessment**, then rework your resume. By knowing yourself, your resume will flow from that knowledge, and you then can articulate successfully your **value** to prospective employers. This is what the rest of the book will help you achieve.

The Resume as a Risk-Reduction Document

"The times are so turbulent, business owners want to keep their risks down. You have to assure them that hiring you is low risk, not high risk." Carol Kleiman, Chicago Tribune

In baseball you get three strikes before you're called **out**. In the business world, you often get only **two**. If you had to replace a key employee because of incompetence, and you replaced that person with someone who also failed to do the job adequately, how would you be perceived by your management? This situation very well may put your career at risk with your employer. For that reason, the hiring executive at all levels usually looks at the resume of potential candidates as a **risk-reduction document**. Therefore, the hiring executive is *not* looking for *less* information (a short resume), but rather *more* information (long resumes, 2-3 pages). The short resume only benefits the HR department by reducing their workload.

Who are Your Customers?

Most people experience frustration during their job search, especially when revising their marketing materials, i.e., their resume. A lot of this confusion is due in part to the conflicting advice people receive, both directly from associates and outplacement counselors, and indirectly from books and articles on the topic. In fact, at last count, there are more than 300 books in print on how to construct and write a resume, and even more online. Much of this information adds to the confusion and frustration, because the starting point from which their discussion is written is based on human resources' hiring viewpoint, *not* the hiring executive's.

Hiring managers and executives are your audience because they have the open position and are capable of hiring you. It is vital that you write directly to them and provide the information they require.

Your marketing resume will provide the answers to the **Three Issues in the Hiring Decision**:
- Can you do the job?
- Will you fit with our team?
- Do you have experience with our type of business problems or issues?

How you contact hiring executives will be discussed fully later in the book. Now it's important to understand the type of information executives require, why they want it, and how to convey this information through your resume, cover letters, thank-you letters and other materials.

Your audience during the job search is not the HR department. It is the hiring influence and other hiring executives. So how do these individuals approach the problem of replacing a key subordinate?

The resume should be viewed by job seekers as a risk-reduction document—and since your window of opportunity with the hiring influence is short, 10 seconds, you must answer the *two critical questions* upfront at the beginning of the resume for your reader: Can you do the job? Will you fit?

Remember the last time you had to replace a key member of your staff, one that reported directly to you. You had to replace this individual because of their inability to do the job. In going through the resume review and the interview process, hiring executives usually concentrate on two themes: Can the candidate do the job technically, and if hired, would he or she be able to get along with me and my management team? On a percentage basis, the latter issue is between 80 to 90 percent of the decision to hire. Yet, **few resumes even attempt to address the critical issue of fit**.

Quick Quiz

Answer True or False

____ Most books on resume construction are written from the HR viewpoint, not the hiring executive viewpoint.
____ Your resume is not a risk-reduction document, the job application is.
____ Company websites listing job openings are managed by the HR department.
____ Your "window of opportunity," the amount of time recruiters spend reading your resume, is 30 seconds to one minute.

Identify two critical questions your resume should answer in the first 10 seconds.

___ Date you graduated?
___ Can you do the job technically?
___ What problems have you solved?
___ Do you require relocation?
___ Is there good chemistry if hired?
___ Are you a job hopper?

Customer #1: External Recruiter

With the exception of a career advisor, the only other person who can make money off you during a job search is the external recruiter. If you have worked with recruiters before, you know that many are very unprofessional, and poor communicators. Usually they only care about earning a placement fee with the least amount of effort. They are basically "pizza delivery people." They obtain a job order, and then attempt to fill the job specifications without deviation.

From a resume standpoint what is the best way to deal with them?

The answer is simple but not obvious. **Do their job for them.** Give recruiters a resume that satisfies the basic information client companies require: 1) Can you do the job technically? 2) Have you solved the type of problems we deal with? and 3) Will you fit as a personality into the management team? If hired, can you save me money and/or make me money? If your resume answers these questions, the recruiter has little to do except verify these three points. And in many cases, this verification can be done over the telephone. They don't even have to interview you in person.

Customer #2: Company Interviewer

Human resources department members often conduct initial interviews because it's their responsibility and they're usually the most experienced interviewers. Their basic objective in the interview is to determine if you will fit into their organization and a particular department. They don't usually try to determine a candidate's technical ability for the job. Line management and the hiring managers do that.

As discussed above, if your resume answers the three critical questions for the executive recruiter, then you have also answered the critical questions HR interviewers will require. In reality, you have created a retained search (headhunter) / contingent (employment agency) resume. You've done the recruiter's job for them. All they have to do is call you and verify what is on the resume. Then they call the client company and take credit for the information presented on your resume. This is the *Second Law of Sales*: Make it easy for the customer to buy.

Making it easy for the customer to buy is also true of the fit / personality issue. When they speak with you on the phone and you match the personality description, and you've confirmed what is on the resume, their comfort level will increase. When they interview you in-person, if you again match the personality description, their comfort level will be reinforced a second time, thus giving you a distinct competitive advantage over other candidates. In addition, and **more importantly**, your resume will allow the HR interviewer to better and more easily represent your credentials to others in the company.

Customer #3: Hiring Influence

An important HR secret in any job market is that senior executives are not trained in interviewing skills and techniques. Therefore, they're usually poor at the interviewing process. They hire based on their gut feelings. In addition, they take few or no notes during the interview. Under these conditions, when you leave an interview with a hiring executive, what is left? Think about this for a moment.

What's left usually is only an impression that will dissipate after a night's sleep. Therefore, if your resume isn't selling you, **it's killing you**. The way to overcome this handicap is to have the answer to the three critical questions fully explained in your resume. Recognize and act on the fact that the resume is a risk-reduction document. Make it easy for people to hire you by reducing their hiring risk.

Additional Hiring Concepts

In most cases, the amount of time your reader will devote to your resume is short. This is what I call your window of opportunity. Since resume responses to ads and Internet postings often number in the thousands, the reader of your resume and cover letter is presented every day with the same problem. With such high volume of responses, they can give each response only a short amount of time—10 seconds. But where to put that time—in the cover letter or in the resume? The reader will put his or her 10 seconds into skimming your resume.

Now take a minute to review your resume. Do you provide the hiring influence with the information to make an informed hiring decision?

1. Can you do the job?
2. Have you solved our type of issues?
3. Will you fit?

If not, are you making it difficult for your customer to buy?

Insider's Tip: Professional recruiters in the Human Resources department and executive recruiters can skim your resume in only 10 seconds. They look for three patterns.

1. Are you a job hopper?

2. Is there a progression in title on the first page? This is the best reference you can have, because it is a testimonial from an employer on how good you are.

3. Is there a progression in salary? The reader of your resume should never get this information from your document. *Leave it off*!

So when HR reviews your resume, it should show at least one progress in job title on the first page. And it will be necessary to try to avoid being perceived as a job hopper.

No Surprises / Full Disclosure

To round out our discussion on how people hire is the issue of **no surprises**. If you have ever managed a department, then chances are that you ran your department based on one basic rule, which you clearly communicated to your subordinates: **no surprises**. If it was good news or bad news, you wanted to receive it first. You could not afford to go into a business meeting with your boss and other members of his management team and be hit with a "surprise." You need to be prepared to discuss any good or bad news. Therefore, you made it crystal-clear to your staff: **no surprises**. You get the news first.

The implication of this is important. The hiring influence runs their department or division the same way that you do: no surprises. Therefore, your resume should have **full disclosure** / complete transparency; i.e., no surprises. Your resume should have all the so-called negatives clearly stated in the document, including age, race, sex, unemployed, dates you graduated from college; lack of degree, certification, industry experience; height and weight, if you are very heavy.

How to place negative issues in your resume, and the philosophy behind it, will be discussed later in the book. This is a sensitive topic, especially for women and minorities. It will be dealt with in great detail. For now, putting negatives on your resume will actually strengthen your confidence during the interview, because if the reader wanted to discriminate against you, they would not have contacted you in the first place and brought you in for an interview.

Hiring Model Summary

- Your audience is the hiring influence or hiring manager, not the HR department.

- The hiring influence has several motivators: Can you do the job and get the monkeys off my back? And, If I hired you, what's in it for me (WIIFM)? Will you fit with my management team?

- The hiring influence sees the resume as a risk-reduction document.

- The hiring influence is not results-oriented but problem-oriented.

- The hiring influence speaks two languages: jargon and numbers.

- The amount of time the hiring influence will give to reading your resume is 10 seconds.

- And finally, the hiring influence runs her or his department based on one concept: **no surprises**.

Critical Strategy

Does this scenario sound familiar? You see a job posting for a position that is a perfect match to your background and experience. It "has your name on it." You answer the ad, get the interview that couldn't go any better, and leave feeling you've landed the job. HR said they would get back to you in a few days. Days turn to weeks and you hear nothing—or they get back to you and say they've selected another candidate who more closely fits their needs.

Most people can't figure out what went wrong.

Here's why the interview process failed you.

If the interviewer is unable to "sell" you to his boss, he won't present you to his boss!

For interviewing managers to represent you to their boss, they always need to answer three critical questions:

1. Can you do the job? What's in it for me?
2. Are you the right chemistry, personality or fit?
3. Have you solved the same type of problems / issues we are experiencing?

Since the resume that landed the interview fails to answer these issues, the interviewer lacks the "sales collateral" to present you to her boss. Managers won't jeopardize their image and reputation with their boss for a candidate who doesn't make it easy for them to sell you.

A principal recruiter at the Spencer Stuart search firm in New York City, when reviewing one of our marketing resumes, made these comments:

- "I wouldn't change a thing."
- "You made the recruiter's job easier."

Therefore, to greatly increase your chances to more quickly land a new position, you *need to do the recruiter's job for them.* Make it easy for the customer to buy, especially recruiters who have extensive networks of potential hiring contacts.

RESUME REVIEW *(Traditional)*

- Written for the wrong audience: This resume is written for Human Resources and company job boards, which are managed by HR.

- Uses short bulleted phrases to communicate your skill set, such as • Project Management or • Staff Training.

- Tries to communicate your accomplishments in bulleted fashion, using only "action" words and/or stating results.

- Omits personality / chemistry / fit in the resume, and assumes you'll communicate this critical information during the interview process.

- Is full of surprises, and lacks transferable skills.

The traditional format is recommended by HR executives because it satisfies the requirements of their Human Resources Information System (HRIS) and reduces the workload on HR personnel. The traditional resume format clearly favors the HR department, not the job-search candidate.

Marketing Resume Review

The marketing resume is heavily anchored in proven sales and marketing concepts, and targets the hiring influence instead of HR.

- Communicates a person's expertise in a full paragraph, using the transferable skill "process."

- Uses a storytelling methodology called PAR anchored with a transferable skill, i.e., the problem, to describe your accomplishments.

- Describes in detail a person's management style and personality that has been verified via 360°feedback from colleagues.

- Provides full disclosure.

* * *

Quiz:

- How many swings at the ball do you get in the business world? __1 __2 __3
- The resume isn't a risk-reduction document. __T __F
- Your customers in the job search are?
  - __T __F   Internal HR Recruiters.
  - __T __F   Hiring Executives
  - __T __F   Employment Agencies & Search Firms
- Who manages a company's open jobs website?
  - __ Finance Dept.
  - __ IT Dept.
  - __ HR Department
- Should your resume do the recruiter's job for them? __Yes __No
- Should you make it easy for the recruiter to represent you? __Yes __No
- Identify the three critical issues in most hiring decisions.
  - ____ provide full disclosure, including graduation dates
  - ____ make it easy for the customer to buy
  - ____ can you do the job technically
  - ____ reduced the hiring risk
  - ____ do their job for them
  - ____ good chemistry
  - ____ great problem solver
  - ____ strong management skills
  - ____ have solved the same type of problems

In the next chapter of our counseling program, we will review your homework assignment that aims to build the basic elements of the marketing resume. Can you skip the homework assignment? Of course, but the resume you prepare will not match the candidate the recruiters speaks with on the telephone, or interviews in person. Stay the course; it works!

* * *

Crux of the Job Search Issue: No one will be hired into important positions that offer advancement and competitive compensation, including bonus, unless they have discovered, defined and then articulated their **value** on their resume and during the interview process. *This is the objective of our program.*

* * *

Answers to Quizzes:

• Answer True or False
1. T 2. F 3. T 4. F

• Identify two critical questions
Can you do the job technically?
Is there good chemistry if hired?

• Quiz
1. two 2. F 3. all three 4. HR Department 5. Yes 6. Yes 7. Can you do the job technically; good chemistry; have you solved the same type of problems?

CHAPTER 5

The Importance of Self-Assessment

If you haven't discovered yourself, neither will anyone else. What do you have to sell that someone will buy?

At a talk I gave in Connecticut, I met the director of international finance for a large consumer-goods corporation. He had just completed six months with a major outplacement firm, without success.

Since many of my concepts resonated with his business experience, he decided to accept my offer for a free consultation. Liking what he heard, and impressed with the sample marketing resume and support materials, he decided to sign up and work with me. Through his connections at the company, he was able to obtain a second outplacement fee. Thus he received the full Career Marketing counseling program at no cost.

During our final counseling session, while reviewing how best to work with executive recruiters, I suggested my client do a major mailing to both domestic and international recruiters.

Soon after, he was contacted by Egon Zehnder International, Inc., a leading executive-search firm. My client commented to me: "They also provided extremely positive feedback on the information content of the resume." Although all my client's experience was entirely in consumer goods, the recruiter then arranged for him to interview with two companies: a $2.5 billion manufacturer of high-tech industrial valves, and a $1.5 billion biotech firm.

In the case of biotech, 300 resumes were screened and four were invited in for the initial interview. All of the interviewees had strong credentials in accounting, and had managed a finance department outside of the United States. Only two were invited back for the second round of interviews.

Using six additional closing documents, including one called "Get the job by doing the job," my client was hired by the biotech firm, despite his total **lack of any industry experience**.

Bottom line: Based on the strength of my client's resume, the recruiter was willing to "think outside the box."

* * *

Creating a resume that sells is impossible without self-assessment. Without it, you can't talk about your background and experience with authority. You can't violate one of the great definitions of luck: preparation meeting opportunity. Experience has shown that opportunities are of little value without the proper preparation. Do you really know the product you're selling? If not, you're not prepared to do anything but waste those opportunities.

The message in your resume must be clear: It doesn't cost you to hire me, it pays! If this message is not clearly communicated to the reader, it's time to stop your job search and take a hard look at your resume.

Your resume won't sell you by highlighting the aspects of your work history that are important to you—unless they match what the hiring executives need to know: Can this person solve the problems our company is facing? Can he or she fit with the rest of my staff? And do you possess the necessary skills?

If you or your resume can't answer those questions, it's killing you. To answer those questions, you need to clearly understand what you bring to the table.

It's not just about getting interviews, it's about closing the sale!

Since an interview is nothing more than a sales call, most candidates will not get the job offer if they don't know the product they're selling. In counseling candidates at all levels, I've found that everyone comes to the counseling process with two basic problems: They don't know the product they're selling, and they don't know what they want to do with the rest of their career. Time for some self-assessment, folks.

Creating a resume that sells is impossible without self-assessment. Without it, you can't talk authoritatively about your background. Experience has shown that opportunities are of little value without the proper preparation. Do you really know the product you're selling? If not, you're not prepared to do anything but waste those opportunities.

Take some time to reflect on your career. In each position, what was it that you did? What issues did you face? What problems did you solve? What was your value? This isn't easy. It's hard to be sure if you've drilled down to the core issues, the basic problems. But it simply must be done if you want to speak the hiring influence's language.

Taking a bad resume and bringing it up to date only creates a bad, up-to-date resume. Without extensive self-assessment—what marketing people call "product knowledge"—many candidates will get the interview, but fail to close the sale.

In summary, start with self-assessment, then rework your resume. The first commandment of navigating your career: Know thyself—your resume will flow from that knowledge, and you then can articulate successfully your value to prospective employers.

* * *

Resume Critique

The primary purpose of the resume review is to provide you with feedback from the buyer's standpoint. This is because it is not what you want to sell that counts in the job search; rather, it is what the hiring executive wants to buy. Key to any successful job search is to learn to think like your customer, the person who can hire you.

An additional purpose of this review is to challenge conventional assumptions, and to get you to question the strategies and tactics that you're using in your job search.

Answer each question honestly:

- Do you lead off with your chin? First thing you say to the reader is that you are at least 40 years old or older. What do you hope to accomplish by doing this? Asking to be discriminated against, based on your age? Wrong approach. European approach; don't use in the United States. __Yes __No

- Does the resume lack eye appeal? Fails to draw the reader into your document. Very crowded. Failure to differentiate yourself from the competition. __ Yes __No

- Are there spelling and punctuation errors or word omissions? __Yes __No

- Lacks a specific focus, or provides a confusing focus? What type of professional is the reader viewing? Administrative, operations, IT, telecommunications, or nonprofit? And at what level? __Yes __No

- On the first page, is the emphasis on your responsibilities, instead of answering the critical question—can you do the job? __Yes __No

- Fails to provide reader with a clear picture of the "playing field," i.e., assumes the reader knows who your employer is, and what industry they are in, their specialty and size. __Yes __No

- Lacks an email address, which says you are not technology current. Email addresses in color assumes a color printer at the other end of your emails. __Yes __No

- Fails to describe the scope of your management responsibilities and your reporting relationship. __ Yes __No

- Uses the wrong resume format. Of the three formats: **inverse chronological**, functional or combination, only the inverse chronological is acceptable to hiring professionals. __Yes __No

- Tries to hide your age by omitting the dates under education. Since most executives manage based on the concept of "no surprises," this is a serious error, especially for senior managers. Big contradiction with the first item above. __Yes __No

Remember: The resume is a risk-reduction document for the reader.

- Fails to mention your education. __Yes __No

- Fails to discuss personal data and interests. Again, the issue of no surprises: 80 to 90 percent of the hiring decision is personality, chemistry and fit. Do I like you and trust you? Do I want to work with you? Understand that people hire in their own image. __Yes __No

- Little or no use of numbers in the document related to your results. A grievous mistake, since the person who will hire you speaks two specific languages: jargon and numbers. An especially serious mistake made by senior managers (financial or nonfinancial). Don't do it. And numbers should look real. __Yes __No

- Fails to describe yourself as a personality and provide a detailed summary of your expertise. From the reader's perspective, **what skill set is the reader buying?** __Yes __No

- Fails to tell the reader what they are buying, i.e., your expertise. A top the first page of your resume, what does project management or sales mean to the reader? If you let the reader jump to a conclusion, they will always jump to a negative one. You may know what the term means, but have you communicated your understanding of it to the reader? __Yes __No

- Gaps or omissions; lies or distortions. Please, no surprises. __Yes __No

- Fails to use the PAR methodology (Problem-Action-Result) to document your value to an employer. __Yes __No

- Fails to play down negative aspects of your work history and expand on positive aspects of your career. __Yes __No

- Locking yourself into a specific industry or subsection of an industry. Strongest prejudice in the job market. This can seriously hurt your career. __Yes __No

- Fails to show a progression in job title on first page. Best reference you can have. __Yes __No

- Visually comes across as a job hopper. __Yes __No

- Use of an objective on your resume. That is 180°wrong. It is not what you want to sell. Rather it is what your customer wants to buy. __Yes __No

- Fails to describe you as a "business person" rather than the best "technical" person for the job. This can be deadly in the job search. __Yes __No

- Resume is too short, especially those work experiences that will sell with a future employer. Unable to "tell your story" adequately. __Yes __No

- Is your resume an engaging read? __Yes __No

- Does it look like everyone else's resume? __Yes __No

- The main weakness in most resumes is the weakness of the **presentation!** If the resume fails to adequately communicate the candidate's **value**—show skills to do the job, **fit** with their management team, and demonstrated ability to solve business problems—then you're making it difficult for the hiring person to buy.

- In addition, using your current resume, is it difficult for an interviewer to "sell" you to their superior? __ Yes __No

* * *

If this resume critique demonstrates weak areas in your "sales presentation," then continue to learn some of the best methodologies developed over the last 28 years.

Critical Issue:

> **"Unless the interviewer can *sell* you to their boss, they won't *present* you to their boss!"**

Will the next position you accept be the next right job for your career, and will it be a strong "work marriage"? Or will you **settle**?

Don't make it difficult for the reader to "buy." Most people fail to answer the key question that forms 90 percent of the basis of the hiring decision: Will you fit if the company hires you? This question should be answered within the first 10 seconds of reading your resume. And yes, executive recruiters are an important audience, and want the answer to the "fit" question also.

As the first law of sales states, it isn't what you want to sell that counts in the hiring equation. Rather, it is what the reader, your customer, wants to buy.

Self-Assess Your Resume

With this new perspective on the resume, conduct a self-analysis using the review below. Answer these questions honestly:

1. Have you defined your skill set / areas of expertise adequately for the reader? Does the skill set described at the top of your resume say to the reader: "Been there, done that?" If not, why not?

    a. *Example*: You may have indicated at the top of your resume that you know business development. But what does it mean to the reader? The reader knows his understanding of business development, but does he know *your* understanding? Probably not.

2. Have you communicated that you can fit into the reader's organization?

3. In your 10-second window of opportunity with the reader, does he or she obtain a clear picture of your skills and personality? Remember, if you allow the reader of your resume to jump to conclusions, they usually jump to negative ones.

4. Is your resume a risk-reduction document? Do you reduce the hiring risk because you provided full disclosure? You're not hiding anything, right?

5. Are most of your responses to job advertisements ending up in the HR department? If so, why are you sending your materials there? Because you didn't know better, or because you are lazy?

If your answers are mostly negative, it will be necessary to rethink your resume and do a comprehensive resume update that answers the three critical questions.

1. Can you do the job technically?

2. Have you solved problems similar to the hiring organization?
3. Will you fit?

Below is an outline of the five-step job search model we're going to use. Carefully review this outline and try to guess where most people would first jump into the model if they just lost their job?

FIVE-STEP JOB SEARCH MODEL

I. Product Analysis / Self-Assessment (most important) Packaging Yourself —P AR methodology, sometimes called branding.

II. Determine Employer's Needs
   A. Want-Ad Analysis

III. Develop Marketing Materials, i.e., match the company's needs with the candidate's experience
   A. Marketing (targeted) Resume
   B. Cover Letters
   C. Direct-Marketing Letters
   D. Other Communications Pieces
      1. Thank-You Letters: 2-4 pages
      2. Disappointment Letter
      3. Networking Outline: 2 pages

IV. Campaign Mechanics
   A. Job Postings / Want Ads
   B. Executive-Search Firms and Employment Agencies
   C. "Hidden" Job Market—65 percent of all open positions
   D. Networking
      1. Written Networking Approach

V. The Interview
   A. Interviewing Backward—A Practical Strategy
   B. Activities Before, During and After the Interview
   C. Evaluating Your Performance in the Interview

If you chose Step III-A, you're correct. The first thing most job seekers do when they lose their job is to update their resume. Since they skipped Steps I and II, they failed to define themselves as a product, and also failed to define their targeted employer's business needs. As a result, the search will be unnecessarily extended and full of frustration. I will help you avoid these common job-search mistakes, but only if you complete Steps I and II before moving on.

Self-Assessment: The Rudder That Steers Your Ship

Just like most products in a saturated market, you must clearly differentiate yourself from the masses. This is accomplished through developing a personal brand.

Your personal brand is your trademark and makes you unique and distinctive from others in your industry and talent pool. Personal branding creates your unique value proposition (UVP) for potential employers and helps set you apart from your competition. In our book, we accomplish this through the use of two transferable skills:

1. Use of **process** to describe your skill set, and

2. Description of how you solved **universal problems** using a **resume** storytelling format.

In both cases, the emphasis is on universal aspects in the business world. As Peter Drucker pointed out:

"Most business issues are generic issues—repetitions of familiar problems cloaked in the guise of uniqueness."

In reviewing the five-step job search model, you'll notice that the first step is self-assessment, or what product managers in industry call product knowledge. The concept is basic: It's very difficult to convince a prospective employer to hire you if you can't articulate your value to the new employer. If you don't know the product you're selling, how can the new employer and its representatives honestly evaluate your future contribution?

Imagine you're in an electronic superstore and ask the salesperson to explain the differences between the current displays of digital video cameras. If the salesperson weren't knowledgeable about these products and unable to explain the pros and cons of each model, you probably would go to another store to make your purchase.

Since the interview is basically a "sales call," it's in your self-interest to know the product you're selling: your skills and experience.

Bottom line: During the job search process, you're selling confidence. Does your resume communicate your confidence adequately? Does it represent your true **value**?

* * *

In a real sense, what you're selling in the interview are two impressions.

1. You're confident. If they hire you for the position, you can do the job.
2. You're also selling peace of mind. If hired, your boss can go on vacation with the assurance that you will do the job and not bother him or her with any phone calls.

Now, the critical question: Where does **confidence** come from? Carol Tavris, in her article "You Are What You Do," *Prime Time*, November 1980, writes "...no immutable 'self' determines what we are, what we think or feel. Our jobs, families, and friends are far more effective than therapy in determining personal growth and change."

Confidence comes from *doing*! Not having a clear and defined picture of your past work experience, and a superior method of communicating that experience, is a great handicap in trying to explain the value you bring to a new employer.

Therefore, the **main objective of this book** is to teach you how to **discover, define and articulate your value to prospective employers**.

Jumping the Gun

The first rule in successful career management is to obtain an understanding of the job market and the universal sales process. For example, it's not what you want to sell that counts, rather it's what the customer wants to buy. Only marketing and sales strategies can fill that bill.

Resist the temptation to skip an understanding of these issues.

When the loss of employment appears imminent, most people jump into the job-search model at Step III-A: They update their resume. They take their old resume—usually a poor document since it fails to answer the three critical questions—and bring it up to date. Skipping the first two steps in the search model results in a revised resume written for an audience that wasn't defined, and describes a product (yourself), also undefined.

Quiz: When you last updated your resume, did you consider these issues? Answer Yes or No.

Who is the hiring audience you're writing to? ____
What qualities, background, education and experience does your audience require? ____
Do you know the product you're selling? ____
What **value** do you bring to your next employer? ____
Can you articulate your expertise or skill set that you're selling? ____
Can you answer the classic question: Tell me about yourself?____

Without defining the product you're selling (Step I), and defining the employer's needs (Step II), the job search will be unnecessarily long, costly, frustrating and probably fail to move your career forward. This is the reason more than 70 percent of the workforce in surveys say they don't like the work they're doing or are underemployed.

Suggestion: Stop settling. Complete Steps I and II in the five-step job search model and give your career a long-overdue competitive advantage.

* * *

JOB SEARCH OUTLINE

I. Define the Product – YOU

A. How to Compete?
   1. Technical content vs. business process
   2. Identify first transferable skill: process
   3. Defining your skill set (areas of expertise) in process terms
B. How to Communicate your **Value**
   1. Introduction to Problem—Action—Result (PAR)
   2. Second transferable skill: Problem
   3. Defining your accomplishments in PAR

II. Define Customer Needs
   A. Basic industry research—Standard & Poor's Industry Surveys
   B. Want-ad analysis technique

III. Develop Marketing Materials (Sales Collateral)
   A. Marketing Resume
   B. Cover Letters—three versions
   C. Written Networking Piece
   D. Elevator and Two-Minute Pitch
   E. Direct Marketing Letters: non-resume strategy
   J. Interview Closing Documents: An Introduction
      1. Thank-You Letters
      2. Skills Match Summary
      3. Project / Deal Sheet
      4. Best Candidate for the Job
      5. How to Use Me
      6. Get the Job by Doing the Job
      7. Disappointment Letter

IV. Job-Search Mechanics
   A. Ads and the Internet
   B. Contingent and Executive-Search Agencies
   C. Hidden Job Market—Direct-Mail Strategies
   D. Networking

V. Interviewing Process
   A. Activities Before the Interview
   B. Activities During the Interview
   C. Activities After the Interview, including Salary Negotiation

* * *

Article:

Self-Assessment

At the crossroads, a forced opportunity, but an opportunity nevertheless.
by Jack Quinn

Who am I now? Alphonse Carr said, "Every person has three characters—that which he exhibits, that which he has, and that which he thinks he has." Who you are now is the sum of your life and work adventures until today. During those years, what challenges have you faced, what were your responses, and what happened? That's who you are—a series of PARs (Problems-Actions-Results).

At this crossroads, the question to ask yourself is: How much of my life and work did I plan, guide and make happen? How much did I allow to be done to me? The right answers to those questions will come from your assessment of yourself, combined with the assessment of you by others. We must accept from others the effects we have generated.

What is my objective? What is my destination on this voyage through the rest of my life? How do I want to be: to look, talk, dress, and behave? How do I want others to see me, as what kind of a person, socially and in business? Where do I want to live, in detail; what do I want? Clothes, cars, stuff? Who will partner? Feel the handshakes, see it happening. Visualize the way you want your life to be happening in sound, motion, color, and with the cast of characters playing the roles you want in your life. That's where I want to go, that's my destination, my objective. See it, hear it, feel it happening—picture it in your mind—in wide-screen, Surround-sound, Technicolor, with you giving your greatest performance among your wonderful cast of characters. Close your eyes and see it. That is no dream. That is your destination, the objective you want to spend your efforts on from now on.

Focus. It is a psychological fact that a person who consistently focuses on an objective will subconsciously make those choices which lead him/her directly or indirectly to it. This is sometimes depicted as the "self-fulfilling prophecy." A sharp, steady and consistent focus on your wide-screen objectives is the "magic" to making those choices that produce the effects you want in your life. Julius Caesar said, "Divide and conquer." Allow exterior influences to lead you into choices incompatible with your objective ,and your focus gets changed, split, fuzzy—you are being divided. Re-sharpening the focus puts you on course.

Doing it. When you know who you are, what your objective is and you keep it consistently in sharp focus—out of reach, but not out of sight—how do you prepare to get there? How do you want your life and work adventures to proceed from today on? **You prepare**. You learn the lessons of *your history;* you listen to the witnesses of your history. PAR your life, PAR the testimony of your witnesses. Construct from your personal and business PARs that representation of you best equipped to reach your objective. That's who you are, who you want to be, who you present to the world.

Getting there. To achieve this kind of long-range personal objective—to make your life come out somewhere near where you'd like it—we have to approach the work we do as a long-range project. In other words, we don't want a job, we want a career. A job and a career are two different animals. In one, you work for a company; in the other, the company works for you. You decide which you want, a job or career, but remember: it takes just as much pain, trouble and effort to lead a bad life as it does to lead a good one. It is up to you which one you want to spend your time on.

Job: *(old English meaning 'lump')* A piece of work, especially, a small miscellaneous piece of work at a stated rate; occasional pieces of work for hire—

or

Career: *(Lat. carrus meaning 'car' or 'cart')* Exercise of activity; **the pursuit of consecutive progressive achievements**, especially, in public, professional or business life; to go at full speed.

INTRODUCTION TO THE HOMEWORK ASSIGNMENT

Defining the Product (You)

Let's start the process of building your new resume. To have a clear understanding, below is an outline of the main elements in the marketing resume. A key characteristic of the marketing resume will be complete transparency / full disclosure and no surprises. This philosophy will be explained later in the book.

Marketing Resume Outline
    Summary of Qualifications:

        Part One: Personality Description (including management style and mission statement)
        Part Two: Areas of Expertise (skill set in process terms)

    Work Experience (in inverse chronological order)

    Military Experience

    Education (with dates of graduation or attendance)

    Special Skills

    Languages

    Affiliations

    Personal Data

    Interests (competitive first)

We'll review each section of the marketing resume and justify why the document is constructed in this fashion. You may agree or disagree, but what we recommend has been tested in the job marketplace for more than 28 years, and it works better than any other format. Full explanations, real-life stories, experiences, and our clients' comments, along with practical exercises, will be found in each chapter as we build the resume.

Building Your Marketing Resume

In reading anyone's resume, the very first piece of information should identify the type of candidate the reader is viewing. Since you only have 10 seconds to capture the reader's attention and only one chance to create a good impression, it is imperative to define yourself within the first few seconds. You do this by using a few choice adjectives and introduce what I call a "handle." For example:

Dedicated, enthusiastic and responsive **sales support / customer service** professional with …

In this example, the handle is "sales support / customer service" professional; it tells the reader precisely what they're holding. The rest of the resume can now be understood more easily because the reader has been provided with a focus (i.e., frame of reference). As the reader continues to review the opening paragraph, it becomes obvious that it's all self-promotional fluff and they skip it. This, however, is exactly the response we're after, because it encourages the reader to use the remaining eight seconds in the next paragraph: skill set / areas of expertise. And this is the section that creates strong credibility with the reader.

So What Are You?

"Trying to define yourself is like trying to bite your own teeth."
          – Alan Watts, English philosopher

Few people can answer the question: What is your skill set or areas of expertise? They will usually give you a blank stare or respond with:

- I sell life insurance
- I'm a teacher
- I'm an IT project manager
- I'm a senior accountant and CPA, or something similar.

The problem with this type of response is:

- it fails to communicate your value
- the terms aren't defined
- it's boring
- people who regularly hire hear it all the time
- it confirms that you don't know the product you're selling

Therefore, to define yourself as a product, you must first study the product via a comprehensive homework assignment.

Quiz: Using numbers 1-5, place the elements of the five-step job search model in the correct sequence.

___Define Employer's Needs ___Interview ___Product Analysis ___Campaign Mechanics
___Develop Marketing Materials

Why a Homework Assignment?

Though it might seem a bit elementary to ask you to complete a homework assignment, experience has shown me that most people don't know the product they're trying to sell. When a prospective client comes in for the initial consultation, I usually ask them two questions:

- _ Where do you want to go next in your career?
- _ What is the skill set / areas of expertise that you are selling?

If you're like most of my clients, you're not sure and are unable to articulate them precisely. Most people, instead of explaining their skills, end up naming *qualities* they think "sell" an employer. For example:

- detail-oriented
- organized
- dedicated
- loyal
- innovative
- collaborative
- resourceful
- entrepreneurial
- precise
- analytical

All these terms describe qualities, *not* skills or expertise. This is just one reason to complete the homework assignment. Other reasons including identifying:

- problems / situations you solved in your work career
- skills you want to take forward in your career
- targeted industries
- your personal mission statement

- your "elevator pitch"
- the title of the person(s) to whom you should be writing
- your responsibilities in each job title
- the size of the budgets you managed
- the number of employees you supervised, directly or indirectly (matrix-managed)
- what's the next "right" position to go after

Therefore, be a good soldier (student), stay the course, and complete the homework assignment below in detail.

An understanding of yourself doesn't just roll off the top of your head. First, you have to locate, then review written documentation from your past work experience, including:

1. old calendars, appointment books or BlackBerries/iPhones/smartphones
2. old performance reviews
3. old correspondence, project notes, reports, proposals or RFPs, studies, presentations, etc.

These materials are located in your closets, attic, basement or garage. We may have thrown out a lot of stuff from previous jobs, but we do keep documentation from experiences we're proud of. Since you need to jog your memory, tear the house apart. You're looking for evidence of:

1. problems you solved
2. accomplishments you're most proud of
3. dollars you made an organization
4. dollars you saved an organization

If you're unsuccessful, the only other alternative is to locate former co-workers and ask them the same four questions above.

Homework Assignment Steps (all support materials are found in the Appendix)

Step 1. Read the two articles from the *Wall Street Journal's National Business Employment Weekly* entitled:

- "Packaging Yourself Like a Proven Product"

- "How Direct Mail Can Excite Hiring Managers"; also in Chapter 14.

Step 2. Read the DVD review

Step 3. Watch the DVD, which is a little over two hours, is indexed and accessible through YouTube. Necessary information is found in the Appendix. Try and watch the DVD with someone who has work experience. Feel free to discuss issues during the viewing. This will make you a more savvy learner and job seeker. Also refer to the handout in the Appendix that supports the DVD presentations.

Quiz: Match the definition for each element of PAR.

Problem ____   Action ____   Result ____

a. tell what, not how
b. universal/generic
c. $, %, time, testimonial

Of the three elements, which is the only one that is believable to all hiring executives? _____

Both the "Action" and "Result" can be fabrications and therefore not believable, because more than 40 percent of information in resumes are distortions or lies, reports Automatic Data Processing (ADP), after reviewing over 2.4 million employment verifications. Recruiters and executives are familiar with this ploy. If the "Problem" in your accomplishment, however, matches the readers' issues—the monkeys on their backs—they need to consider speaking to you via phone or interview, to pick your brain for free consulting.

You just completed the easy part of the homework assignment; now for the more challenging sections. The written part of the assignment is more difficult, because most people have failed to document their accomplishments during the many positions they held in their career. That's why during your annual performance review, your boss only remembered your screw-ups, and you were unable to rebut, because that's all you remembered. Work hard at recalling your accomplishments. This book will give you techniques to help remember your achievements.

Resume Preparation Control Worksheet

Instructions: To create a strong, professional resume that "sells," and which accurately reflects your skills, experience and **value**, this exercise will require your direct input.

Complete the sections and accompanying sheets in as much detail as possible. Save your notes and have them available for subsequent counseling steps.

LIST 1:

Areas of Expertise (your skill set):

Typical examples include project management, sales, product development, accounting, relationship management, executive assistant, etc. Below is the selection list. To obtain a sample in paragraph form, select a total of six topics from the list below which represent those skills that you wish to take into future jobs. Then go to the expanded list in the Appendix entitled "Areas of Expertise," and select those paragraphs that match your desired expertise.

Remember, in making your selection, choose those skill areas that represent where you wish to take your career in the future.

Job Category / Skill Selection List *(See "List #3—Accomplishments—Sample Areas of Expertise by Job Category," in the Appendix)*

Accounting—Advertising & PR—Analytics—Auditing—Banking—Benefits—Brokerage—Business Development—Consulting—Engineering—Events Management—Executive Assistant—Financial—Financial Risk Management—General Management—Human Resources—Insurance—International—Internet—Legal—Logistics/Purchasing— Marketing—Medical—Mergers & Acquisitions—Nonprofit—Operations—Portfolio Management—Product Management—Project Management—Quality—Real Estate—Relationship Management—Research–Brokerage—Sales—Scientific—Self-Employed/Own Business—Social Work—Systems–Low-Level—Systems—Tax—Telecommunications—Trading—Training—Treasury—TV–Radio—Writing & Public Relations

An example of a job category, Information Technology *(Systems)*, is below.

Job Category	Job Title
Information	Systems (Area of Expertise)

Technology   Analyst

Here are several other examples:

Job Category	Job Title
Financial	Controllership
Marketing	Product Marketing
Brokerage	Trading
Health Care	Medical Center Operations
Pharmaceutical	Clinical Data Analyst
Office Management	Administrative Assistant
Human Resources	Director
Nonprofit	Social Work

See the Appendix for the job category and job title that most closely matches your experience.

LIST 2:

Describe Yourself: Use adjectives, verbs or phrases. Typical examples include: hands-on, astute, decisive, creative, results-oriented, versatile, quietly assertive, precise, etc. Use separate sheet in Appendix and select only 10 terms from the list of 50 terms. Also provide the list to 5-8 people with whom you worked/volunteered, who will give you honest feedback. Then match your 10 terms with the summary of your co-workers' responses.

Past Work Experience: Use data contained in old resumes, plus new information, to update your resume and include all dates of employment (full disclosure).

Then, in one sentence, provide a summary describing each of your employers. For example: **The Wing Company**, a division of Adams Industries Inc. (privately held), Cranford, N.J., engaged in the manufacture of heating and ventilation equipment, with sales of $13 million.

Next, provide a brief summary statement of your areas of responsibility in each job title for each employer.

IT example: As a Contract Consultant, responsible for the maintenance and compliance of the Sample Application Management System. Supervised three professionals and reported to Associate Director of IT.

HR example: Managed HR and employee relations programs, including: COBRA, FMLA, health and dental benefits, 457K retirement plan, employee orientation, open enrollment, HRIS, and short- and long-term disability. Assisted in recruiting, training, and employee safety programs. Reported to Manager of Human Resources.

Operations (Retail): Responsible for managing daily operations of $13-$18 million store business units. Administered human resources, including talent evaluation, hiring/coaching/training, payroll and controllable expense budget. Led and facilitated corporate issue phase changes, pricing strategies, and merchandising structure. In addition, analyzed P&L, including inventory control and product flow, loss prevention and risk management. Managed 4-11 Department Heads, 60-200 support employees and reported to Assistant Store Director or Store Director.

LIST 3:

Accomplishments:

List your major accomplishments for each employer. Be sure to include everything within the last 10-12 years, including work done as part of a team project, significant assignments completed for not-for-profit organizations, etc., and take credit for all work performed, including assignments submitted under a name other than your own. Put the greatest amount of your effort into this part of the "homework" assignment.

Definition of accomplishments: 1. Problems solved. 2. Most proud of. 3. Dollars saved. 4. Dollars earned.

EDUCATION: Include specialized courses taken, special honors, awards. State percentage of your education that was financed by scholarships or yourself. Also, in what areas are you self-taught ?

LANGUAGES: Foreign; computers—hardware, software, operating systems and applications.

PERSONAL DATA: Marital status, health, percent you are willing to travel, and whether you're willing to relocate.

INTERESTS: State competitive first (golf, baseball), then noncompetitive activities (fishing, travel, gardening, home repair, etc.).

Most people counseled over the years have taken between one and two weeks to complete the homework assignment. If you have good documentation, you can usually finish the assignment within one week. If your documentation is poor or nonexistent, then it will take longer; usually two to three weeks.

Concerns About Completing the Homework

Question: What if I don't have good documentation from my work experience? **Answer:** Even without appointment books or performance reviews from previous jobs, reading the articles and reviewing the samples in each chapter will jog memories sufficiently to provide enough material to create a strong resume and cover letters.

Question: What if I don't have people I can contact for feedback who know me in a work context and who will keep my job search confidential? **Answer:** Use people you know from nonprofit situations. For example, if you coach a sport, use other coaches; if you're on a civic or religious committee, use other committee members, etc.

Question: Won't people be bothered with my requests for help? **Answer:** Most people make few, if any, comments on your skill set (areas of expertise) list. But most people will spend a few moments to complete the adjectives sheet to help focus your resume and build personality into the document. Most importantly, however, you're giving people the **opportunity** to help you—and one of the most overlooked aspects of human nature is that people **like** to help, especially Americans. It makes them feel good inside. Think about yourself and how you feel when you can take a few moments of your time to aid a friend or acquaintance. People truly like to help, and you will be surprised and cheered by the response.

Question: Does your program require a commitment of time that I can't make? **Answer:** Though most clients take 1-2 weeks to complete the homework, we often have clients who gather the necessary information in as little as 2-3 **days**. The issue is not the quantity of information, but rather the quality. A combination simply of what is currently covered in your resume and what is contained in your memory is often sufficient to complete the program successfully and within a reasonable time frame.

Counseling Program Summary

1. Readings
   a. Two reprints from *The Wall Street Journal*.
   b. Custom-written articles for self-help groups contained throughout the book.

   Topics covered:
   1. Importance of Presentation
   2. Converting Mere Accomplishments into Transferable Skills
   3. Obstacles in the Job Search
   4. Networking
   5. Job-Search Overview

2. Watch dual-disc DVD with accompanying handout

3. Develop three lists.
   a. Identify the top six skill sets (Areas of Expertise). Refer to the custom examples in the Appendix for skills that are organized by functional area, such as programmer or administrative assistant. These samples are all from actual completed resumes.
   b. Develop list of adjectives that describe how other people you worked with saw you (360° feedback instrument).
   c. Develop a list of accomplishments under each job title, for each employer in the Problem - Action - Result (PAR) method. Go back 10-15 years. Refer to the custom examples in the Appendix for accomplishments organized by job title.

4. It takes people who aren't currently employed between one and two weeks to complete the homework assignment. Full-time employees usually take between two and three weeks. Then they're ready for the one-on-one counseling program.

Answers to Quizzes:

• Resume Critique: There are no right answers. Just be sure to answer questions honestly.

- Quiz – Five-Step Job Search Model

    2, 5, 1, 4, 3

- Match the definition for each element of PAR

    Problem = b   Action = a   Result = c

CHAPTER 6

HOW DO I GET FAMILIAR WITH THE MARKETING RESUME?

What's a marketing resume? Is that different from my current resume?

While giving a presentation to the New Jersey chapter of Financial Executives International, I opened my presentation by asking the group two questions: 1) Do you honestly feel that, if you can get the interview with the hiring executive, you would be able to close the sale? Get the job offer? Everyone raised his or her hand in agreement. And 2) by a second show of hands, I asked how many were getting interviews but not getting job offers? Again, everyone's hands went up. It's those trees again—messing up the view of the forest.

The marketing resume uses a **fundamentally different paradigm** that ensures employers can quickly and accurately assess your fit.

- Your technical abilities are clear.
- Your ability to solve problems similar to the hiring executive's is readily apparent.
- Your true work personality is accurately reflected.

Using a marketing resume gets you:
- Noticed and interviewed more often.
- More offers at better compensation.

* * *

When a reader picks up your resume, he or she must know immediately what type of worker he or she is holding. If your resume lacks a focus, you have lost the reader, and she/he will toss your resume. So let's begin by defining who you are, in a way that allows your reader to focus immediately.

Resume Purpose

It's a mistake to think of your resume as a history of your past, as a personal statement, or as some sort of self-expression. Sure, most of the content of any resume is focused on your job history—but written with the intent to create interest, to persuade the employer to call you. The resume is a tool with one specific purpose: to win an interview. A resume is an advertisement for yourself: nothing more, nothing less.

A great resume doesn't just tell what you've done, but also makes the same assertion common to all effective ads: If you buy this product, you will get these specific, direct benefits. It convinces the employer that you have what it takes to be successful in this position or career. **Bottom line**: Your resume needs to inspire prospective employers to pick up the phone and ask you to come in for an interview.

Here is a comment from one of our clients, C.P.F., an assistant managing editor of a magazine and website:

> "I wanted to let you know it was the resume that got me the job. The head of the company saw it and immediately called me in. He said that he had never seen such a well-written resume and that he had to hire me. The whole staff reviewed the resume and decided they wanted me. The head of the company said in 20 years, he had never seen such a perfect resume."

And if you complete this book, you might be able to write something similar.

Outline of Marketing Resume Elements
Summary of Qualifications:
    Part One: Focus and Personality Description (including management style)
    Part Two: Areas of Expertise (Skill Set)
Business / Work Experience (in inverse chronological order)
Military Experience (laid out like regular employment)
Education (with dates of graduation or attendance)
Special Skills
Affiliations (include leadership roles)
Languages (working knowledge or fluency)
Personal Data (cover travel and/or relocation)

Interests (competitive first, then noncompetitive)

There are as many theories and approaches to resume construction as there are people on this planet. And in this life, everyone is an expert in two areas: how to raise a child (after all, you only need to have raised a child once to be an "expert"), and how to construct a winning resume. Here, all you need to qualify as an "expert" is to have had your resume land you a job. Well, if it worked for you, it should work for others. Right? Not necessarily.

Myth: Recruiters will generally spend two or three minutes reading your resume.

Reality: Job advertisements typically draw hundreds or thousands of responses. Recruiters receive 100 to 250 or more resumes a day. Therefore, you have only 10 seconds of the reader's time. That is the sum total of your "window of opportunity." Since they have so little time to read resumes, they skim them. The reader, an HR recruiting or hiring executive, looks for only four patterns: 1) Do you live locally? Few companies want the expense of relocating a candidate. 2) Is the person a job hopper? They review job dates. 3) Is there a progression in job title and responsibility/salary? 4) Who have you worked for? These patterns can be identified by skimming your resume. Yet, most people agonize for long periods of time, writing and revising their resume.

WHAT'S WRONG WITH THE TRADITIONAL RESUME FORMAT?

The traditional resume format has the following problems, which are at first, not obviously, *problems:*
- It is written for the wrong audience: Human Resources and company job boards, which are managed by HR.
- It uses short, bulleted phrases to communicate your skill set, such as project management or strategic marketing plans.
- It tries to communicate your accomplishments in bulleted fashion, using only "action" words and/or stating results.
- It omits personality / chemistry / fit in the resume, and assumes you'll communicate this critical information during the interview process.
- It's full of surprises!

The traditional format is recommended by HR executives because it satisfies the requirements of their Human Resources Information System (HRIS) and reduces the work load on HR recruiters. The traditional resume format clearly favors the HR department, not the job-search candidate.

WHY YOU SHOULDN'T BE *TRADITIONAL*: The Marketing Resume Model

For many years, I've promoted a "sales and marketing approach" to resume preparation, because *the person that gets hired is* not *the person who is best qualified,* but rather the person who is *perceived* to be the best qualified. **It is not reality that counts, but rather, perception**.

Since the job search is a sales problem, it is very important to make it easy for the customer to buy. I have successfully prepared the resumes and counseled more than 3,000 clients across most industries and job categories. Their success has been terrific (see clients' resume comments in the Appendix).

The marketing resume model depends heavily on the use of transferable skills, and has the following elements:

- **Audience**: This resume is written for the hiring influence: presidents, owners, "C-suite" executives, department managers and executive recruiters.
- **Skill set**: Explained in full paragraphs and in process terms (transferable skills); step one, step two in the process. The elements are in the proper sequence and with the proper jargon.
- **Accomplishments**: Described in full paragraphs using the PAR method/storytelling techniques: Problem (transferable skill)—Action—Result.
- **Personality**: An important element in the resume; described using a full paragraph. It is, however, based on 360° feedback from people with whom you worked.

Since 40 to 45 percent of information in resumes has been shown to be either lies or distortions (according to an ADP study), the reader of your resume will be very skeptical of what you claim in your document. Readers simply won't believe you when you say that you know "strategic planning." Without an explanation of your understanding of strategic planning, readers can assume whatever they want. You're depending on an act of faith; i.e., that the reader of your resume will assume that you, a total stranger, are telling the unvarnished truth.

Likewise, the action and result portions of your accomplishments also require an act of faith. So the net effect of using the traditional resume model is that your resume fails to satisfy the informational requirements of those people who can interview and hire you.

As George Bernard Shaw said: "The greatest problem with communication…is the illusion that it has been accomplished."

Quiz: Identify the characteristics of the Marketing Resume:

___ Written for the HR department ___ Written for the job boards

___ Accomplishments are in storytelling format ___ Uses little or no jargon

___ Hiring executives are your audience ___ Your skill set is fully explained
___ Uses short phrases to explain your expertise ___ Communicates in bulleted phrases
___ Uses personality based on 360°feedback ___ Uses full transparency, no surprises
___ Skill set is described in process terms ___ Each accomplishment starts with a problem
___ Accomplishments should start with action words ___ It's full of surprises

THE MARKETING RESUME—A Recruiter's Dream

Our marketing resume is heavily anchored in proven sales and marketing concepts, and targets the hiring influence instead of human resources.

When people lose their job, they sometimes receive company support through outplacement consulting firms. Keep in mind, however, who pays the outplacement firm: HR. Any company that fires you should not be allowed to choose your doctor, your lawyer, or your outplacement service. They cannot be counted on to have your best interests at heart.

HOW IMPORTANT IS THE RESUME?

You don't have to be reminded about the size and quality of the competition you face when applying for a new position. In most industries, the quantity of the applicants has never been greater, and is of excellent quality. The issue then is how to deal with this situation; how to compete successfully?

(See article entitled: "How Important Is a Resume" in the Appendix.)

Understand that you **can't compete in technical terms**. Someone will always have better credentials, better education, more impressive employers, and still be currently employed.

SO HOW BEST TO COMPETE?

To successfully compete in this tough job market, use **presentation**, not additional education or certification. Prepare a resume that satisfies the business needs of employment agency recruiters, executive search recruiters, and hiring executives. Remember, your competition is following the traditional human resources model for resume construction, not the marketing / recruiter's model, which uses two types of transferable skills: process and problems. By switching models, you can achieve a significant competitive advantage.

How important is the resume? Answer: Critical!

1. The resume is the basis of a person's confidence level during the job search and interviewing process. A person who is proud of his/her work history, and how it is reflected in his/her

resume, is always more willing to distribute the document to recruiters, at networking events, and at interviews, because the individual is coming from **a position of strength through self-knowledge**.

The marketing resume format:
- helps increase your self-confidence.
- helps get you focused, be better able to express your skill set, your expertise and accomplishments.
- makes it easier to take ownership of your resume
- and most important, better enables you to **easily** communicate your **value**.

2. If the interviewer can't sell you as a candidate to her boss, she won't present you to her boss. And this **most critical concept** does not come from job search literature. Instead, it comes from sales literature, specifically Neil Rackham's book, *SPIN Selling*.

"Most people with experience in major-account selling would agree with this analysis. It's obvious that a lot of selling goes on when you're not around, so the better you prepare your internal sponsors, the easier it will be for them to convince others in the account." (p.85-6)

Think about this for a moment.
This is why you see a perfect job and it has "your name on it." You answer it and get the interview, which goes exceeding well; then nothing happens. What's going on? The interviewer may like you and think that you're the best candidate, but if the interviewer can't sell you to his boss, he won't embarrass himself by trying to do so. Instead, he would present those candidates that make it easier for him to do the selling.
So how is the selling done? No surprise here!

3. All hiring decisions are based on three factors, and they are the same three factors you consider during those situations in your career when you had to make a hiring decision. You first asked:
- Can the candidate do the job technically? If the candidate could not do the job in technical terms, you skipped this candidate and went on to the next resume. If the candidate demonstrated the ability to do the job, you the asked yourself the second question.

- Has the candidate solved the same type of issues that our department is facing? If the candidate didn't demonstrate experience solving the issues your department was facing, you skipped this resume. If the candidate passed this hurdle, the final question you asked constitutes 90 percent of all hiring decisions at the medium and senior level:
- Do I like you? Will you fit in with our management team? Is there good chemistry?

Now ask yourself this question.

Does your resume answer these three questions, and specifically, do you answer the technical question within the first six to 10 seconds of reading your resume? For the great majority of your competition, the answer is no. By answering the technical question for your reader in six to 10 seconds, you can easily gain an important competitive advantage.

Quiz: Resume Choices: Place the number representing the resume characteristic under the correct resume format.

Characteristic	**Format**
1. Uses Action-Result Methodology	Traditional Resume
2. Skill set written in full paragraphs	
3. Audience: HR department	_____
4. Is full of surprises	_____
5. Uses Problem-Action-Result (PAR)	
6. Uses a full paragraph describing "personality"	
7. Provides full disclosure, no surprises	Marketing Resume
8. Uses bulleted phrases	
9. Audience: hiring executive and external recruiters	
10. Omits personality completely	_____

True or False:

If the interviewer can't sell you to the boss, he or she won't present you to her boss!____

The best way to compete is in technical terms.____

The greatest problem with communications…is the illusion that it has been accomplished.____

The resume is not critical to a job candidate's confidence level. ____

The IT department, not the human resources department, manages a company's daily website activity.

You should construct your resume from the perspective of your customer, the hiring influence. ____

The marketing resume isn't just for people in marketing. ____

* * *

The message in your resume must be clear: It doesn't cost you to hire me, it pays!

Most resumes fail to adequately sell prospective employers for several reasons:

First, your expertise is in your chosen field—not the job search and self-promotion areas. You're used to telling (PowerPoint presentations), not selling. A long time ago, a Walt Kelly comic strip character named Pogo said it best: "We have met the enemy and he is us." An even *longer* time ago, Abraham Lincoln put it a bit more bluntly: "The attorney who tries his own case has a fool for a client." A marketing executive client of mine really summed it up: "I can market anything except, it seems, myself." He was too close to "it" (his career) to differentiate clearly between what sells to prospective employers and what is meaningful to the candidate.

In taking a look at your resume, you'll probably see a lot of accomplishments that are there for the wrong reason. Your resume won't sell you by highlighting the aspects of your work history that are important to you—*unless* they're the same things that hiring executives *need* to know: Can this person solve the problems our company is facing? Can he or she fit with the rest of my staff?

If you or your resume can't answer those questions, it's killing you. And to answer those questions, you need to have a clear understanding of what it is that you bring to the table. It's not just a question of getting the interview; it is a question of closing the sale. Since an interview is really a sales call, most job seekers will not get the job offer if they don't know the product they're selling. In counseling clients at all levels for the past 28 years, I've found that everyone comes to the counseling process with two basic problems: They don't know the product they're selling, and they don't know what they want to do with the rest of their career. Time for some self-discovery, folks.

Creating a resume that sells is impossible without some self-assessment. Without it, you can't talk about your background and experience with authority. You can't violate one of the great definitions of luck: preparation meeting opportunity. Experience has shown that opportunities are of little value without the proper preparation. Do you really know the product you're selling? If not, you're not prepared to do anything but waste those opportunities.

Take some time to reflect on your career. In each position, what was it that you did? What issues did you face? What problems did you solve? What was your *value*? This isn't easy. It's hard to be sure if you haven't drilled down to the core issues, the basic problems. But it simply must be done if you want to speak the hiring manager's language.

By knowing yourself, your resume will flow from that knowledge, and you can then articulate successfully your **value** to prospective employers.

Harder Than Learning the New Concepts is Forgetting the Old

On June 16, 1993, Michael Eisen, a staff sportswriter for the *Star-Ledger* wrote an article on the new coach for the New York Giants football team titled "After 14 Seasons With Giants, Simms Is Learning a New System." The quote below is from that article.

> "(Phil) Simms knew that system as well as anyone. And he admits to having his share of problems learning (Dan) Reeve's scheme. 'It was terrible at first,' he said. "It's not so much learning the new offense, it's forgetting the old one. That was by far the hardest thing."

This concept applies in spades to the job search. Unfortunately, when a person comes to a job search, they bring a lot of baggage with them—old experiences and a lot of bad information about how to prepare your resume and conduct the search. To use an analogy, if your brain is a chalkboard, the problem is not writing new information on the board; rather, it is erasing the chalkboard first, then writing the new job search information. Based on my experience as a career counselor and coach, the only way to rid yourself of this old baggage is to hear the new ideas and strategies several times and to apply the concepts to your new marketing resume and job-search effort.

Forgetting the old way to prepare your resume is the biggest difficulty you will have to overcome in learning our strategies and methods!

SUMMARY QUIZ

WHAT DO YOU KNOW ABOUT RESUMES?

1. What a resume is not.
    a. An essay on your work history ____
    b. A personal autobiography ____
    c. An introduction to an employer ____
    d. An employment application ____

2. Of the three types of resumes, which one is preferred by recruiters?
    a. Inverse chronological ____
    b. Functional ____
    c. Combination (first page functional and second page chronological) ____

3. The crux of the job search issue is that it is a sales problem. True ____ False ____

4. If you answered true to the above question, who are the salespersons in your job search; who will help sell you into a new position?
   a. Yourself ____
   b. Human resources/personnel recruiters ____
   c. Agency recruiters ____
   d. Hiring executives ____
   e. Business contacts ____
   f. Networking contacts ____
   g. All of the above ____

The questions below should be answered either true or false.

5. Your resume is a means of packaging your relevant work and educational experience. ____
6. Your resume is a sales presentation that attempts to sell a product: YOU. ____
7. Your resumes should cause you to get more interviews than the competition, because the theme of your resume is that "it doesn't cost to hire you, it pays." ____
8. Price is only an issue in the absence of value! ____
9. Though employers advertise for a "generalist," they usually only hire specialists who can solve business problems. ____
10. Your resume should present facts in a carefully selected manner. It should tell a complete story with no surprises. ____
11. Your resume is written for a specific, well-defined audience: the human resources department. ____

12. The language of the person who will hire you is to make or save money. ____
13. Your resume should use three languages: English, jargon, and numbers. ____
14. You should put your personality on the resume, because managers hire in their own image. ____
15. To focus your reader, you should begin your resume with an objective. ____
16. The length of your resume shouldn't exceed one page, which makes it easier for HR executives. ____

17. You should hide your age by omitting the dates under education. ____
18. There should be little or no use of numbers in your accomplishments. ____
19. "The greatest problem with communication…is the illusion and it has been accomplished." ____
20. You can come across as a job hopper. ____
21. It is important to show a progression in job title on the first page of your resume. ____

22. Hiring, recruiting, and HR executives can evaluate your resume in 10 seconds. ____

23. The preferred strategy in your resume is to present yourself as the best technical person for the job. ____

24. People always have two job titles at the same time: a payroll title and their functional title. ____

25. Your resume should only cover the last 10 years of your work history. ____

26. Your resume emphasis should try and "lock" yourself into one specific industry. ____

27. Your skill set should be brief, and arranged in short columns with bullets and positioned at the top of the first page of your resume. ____

28. The end of your resume should contain your personal data and interests. ____

29. Each key position in your resume should describe your management responsibilities, i.e., "the playing field." ____

30. Your resume should have a high appeal, draw the reader into the document, and be an engaging read. ____

31. Your resume should not differentiate yourself from the competition. It is better not to stand out from the crowd. ____

32. You should use a picture of yourself on the resume like they do in Europe. ____

33. On the first page, your emphasis should be about your responsibilities and job titles instead of your accomplishments. ____

34. Any prejudices you may be facing, including age, sex, race, national origin, or being out of work, should be on your resume. ____

35. Your resume should begin with your education, especially if you went to a top school and , received awards and/or held leadership positions. ____

36. The resume is a "risk-reduction document" for the hiring person. ____

37. The best reference you can have is to show a progression in job title on the first page. ____

38. The person reading your resume wants full disclosure, no surprises. ____

39. The best methodology for documenting your value is to tell a complete story through Problem–Action–Result. ____

40. To avoid scams, it is best to leave off your address; only use your name and telephone number. ____

* * *

Answers to Quizzes:

*Quiz: Identify characteristics of the marketing resume
- Accomplishments are in storytelling format

113

- Hiring executives are your audience
- Your skill set is fully explained
- Uses personality-based 360° feedback
- Uses full transparency
- Skill set is described in process terms
- Each accomplishment starts with a problem

Resume Choices

Traditional Resume: 1, 3, 4, 8, 10

Marketing Resume: 2, 5, 6, 7, 9

True or False: T, F, T, F, F, T, T

Summary Quiz

1. a, b, d 2. a 3. T, 4. g, 5. T, 6. T, 7. T, 8. T, 9. T, 10. T, 11. F, 12. T, 13. T, 14. T, 15. F, 16. F, 17. F, 18. F, 19. T, 20. F, 21. T, 22.T, 23. F, 24. T, 25. F, 26. F, 27. F, 28. T, 29. T, 30. T, 31. F, 32. F, 33.F, 34. T, 35. F, 36. T, 37. T, 38. T, 39. T, 40. F.

CHAPTER 7

WHY A HOMEWORK ASSIGNMENT?

If you're going to be first team, you need to practice, practice, practice.

The best strategy for forgetting the old way of preparing your resume is to replace it with a different strategy. Below is the step-by-step process that I have used successfully. If you faithfully follow these steps, you will be able to create the marketing resume and greatly strengthen your confidence level and interviewing abilities. The process will, in effect, teach you **personal selling skills**.

MATERIALS FOR THE HOMEWORK ASSIGNMENT[**]:

   A. Resume Preparation Control Sheet and Documentation Trail

   B. Article: Packaging Yourself Like A Proven Product

   C. Article: How Direct Mail Can Excite Hiring Managers

Helping Clients Define and Articulate Their Value

Dual DVD on YouTube (see Appendix)
   1. The Hiring Model and PAR Methodology
   2. Advanced Interviewing Skills and Direct Mail Strategies

List of Instructions

Assignment Control Sheet

Areas of Expertise List

Example—Areas of Expertise for Program / Project Management

Model Cover Letter for 360° feedback

Adjectives / Survey Feedback Sheet

How to Organize Your Notes

Documenting Your Value—Accomplishments List

PAR Quiz

Past Work Experience—Frito-Lay Sample

How Problems Are Solved

** *Copies of all support materials are at the end of the chapter or in the Appendix.*

Below is a comprehensive outline of the counseling-process steps required to create the necessary information for the marketing resume.

Step 1. Read two articles from the *National Business Employment Weekly* of *The Wall Street Journal*.

- "Packaging Yourself Like a Proven Product"
- "How Direct Mail Can Excite Hiring Managers"

Step 2. Below are the essential articles you will need to read to maximize the program's benefits. Read articles 1, 2, and 3. Read article 4 if appropriate. These articles are located in the Appendix.

1 – "Think Like Your Customer"
2 – "How Important Is the Resume?"
3 – "Break Out of Your Industry"
4 – "Negotiating an Outplacement Agreement"

Step 3. Read DVD Review.

Step 4. Watch the dual DVD, which is on YouTube. See Appendix.

Step 4. Resume Preparation Control Worksheet.

Instructions: To create a strong, professional resume that "sells," and which accurately reflects your skills, experience and **value**, this program will require your direct input.

Complete the sections below in as much detail as possible. Save your notes and have them available for subsequent counseling steps. To stay organized while working on your homework, use a looseleaf binder with separators.

List 1:

Areas of Expertise / **Skill Set** (Sample Areas of Expertise by Job Category are located in the Appendix.)

Typical examples include project management, executive assistant, sales, product development, accounting, application systems support, relationship management, etc. You have to limit your selection to a total of six topics for inclusion in the marketing resume. In selecting, choose those skill areas in which you're strong *and* that represent where you wish to take your career.

* * *

Counseling assistance is available from **Career Marketing Consultants** to help you develop your areas of expertise. The list of 51 categories below contains sample areas of expertise topics. Each category has five or more examples that allow you to "cut and paste" when developing your own skill set. All the examples are in **process terms**—one of the two critical transferable skills.

* * *

Job Category / Skill Selection List

Accounting.doc

Accting-BusDev.doc

Advertising & PR.doc

Analytics.doc

Application.doc

Audit.doc

Banking.doc

Benefits.doc

Brokerage.doc

Business Development.doc

Consulting PARs.doc

Consulting.doc

Engineering.doc

Events Management.doc

Executive Assistant.doc

Expertise —Telecom.doc

Expertise—Corp.Communi.doc

Financial Risk Mgmt.doc

Financial.doc

General Management.doc

Human Resources.doc

Insurance.doc

International.doc

Internet.doc

Legal.doc

Logistics/Purchasing.doc

Marketing.doc

Medical.doc

Mergers & Acquisitions.doc

Nonprofit.doc

Operations.doc

Portfolio Expertise.doc

Product Management.doc

Project Management.doc

Quality.doc

Real Estate.doc

Relationship Management.doc
Research—Brokerage.doc
Sales & Mktg.doc
Scientific.doc
Self-Employed.doc
Social Work.doc
Strategy.doc
Systems—Lower Level.doc
Systems.doc
Tax.doc
Trading.doc
Training.doc
Treasury.doc
TV/Radio.doc
Writing & Public Relations.doc

List 2

Describe yourself, your management style and personality (details in Chapter 10)

You're Too Close to the Product You're Selling

Most people lack objectivity and have little experience writing about themselves. Besides, few of us ever receive critical and meaningful feedback on our work performance. Many of us go through major parts of our career without ever getting a formal, written performance review.

Many people, when they take a job interview, usually "retreat to the familiar" and wing it. Without self-assessment, it is very difficult to talk about your background and experience with authority. In reality, during the interview you are "selling confidence": the ability to take the interviewer's problems off his or her back and put it on yours! Remember, you can't violate Vince Lombardi's definition of **luck**: Preparation meeting opportunity.

My many years of counseling experience have convinced me that opportunities are of little value without the proper preparation. Ask yourself these questions:

- Do you really know the product you're selling?
- Can you articulate your value?

To be able to answer these questions during an interview, complete the homework assignment and then continue to develop your marketing resume.

List 3
Past Work Experience

In developing the largest section of any resume, it's important to use data contained in old resumes, plus new information to update your resume. This includes all dates of employment.

Provide a one-sentence summary describing each employer. For example: THE WING COMPANY, a division of Adams Industries Inc. (privately held), Cranford, N.J., engaged in the manufacture of heating and ventilation equipment with sales of $13 million. Next, provide a brief summary statement of your areas of responsibility *in each job title* for each employer.

Next, list your major **accomplishments** under each appropriate job title for each employer. Be sure to include everything within the past 10 to 15 years, including work done as part of a team project, significant assignments completed for not-for-profit organizations, and credit for all work performed, including assignments submitted under a name other than your own.

Definition of accomplishments: 1. Problems solved. 2. Most proud of. 3. Dollars saved. 4. Dollars earned.

Go to any written documentation that you still have, including:
   a. Old calendars, appointment schedules, or smartphones.
   b. Old performance reviews, if any.
   c. Old correspondence, project notes, reports, proposals or RFPs, studies, PowerPoint presentations, drawings.

Should your written documentation be lacking, talk to people you worked with in the past and ask them the same questions that you have to answer in the "accomplishments" section above:

   a. What problems / issues did you solve?
   b. What are you most proud of?
   c. Did you save the organization money?
   d. Did you make money for the organization?

121

And finally, review physical evidence from your office or desk; then look in your basement, attic, closets, and garage. Since most people keep what they're proud of, don't be surprised if some valuable information turns up for use in the homework assignment.

MILITARY EXPERIENCE

This experience is valid "work" experience, and should be treated the same as other work experiences. That is, describe the particular branch of the military (Army, Navy, Marines, Air Force, Coast Guard); the division you were assigned to (infantry, artillery, transportation, etc.); and what you managed in terms of budgets, equipment, and personnel, along with your reporting relationship. Like regular work experience, accomplishments are described using the storytelling method: Problem—Action—Result (PAR).

EDUCATION: Include specialized courses taken, special honors, awards. State percentage of your education that was financed by scholarships or yourself. Also include self-taught knowledge.

AFFILIATIONS: List organizations you belong to, and any leadership positions held.

LANGUAGES: Include all foreign-language ability, such as read, write and speak the language fluently, or working knowledge of the language. For computer languages, include the hardware, software, operating systems and applications, if appropriate.

PERSONAL DATA: Include marital status, health, percentage you are willing to travel, and whether you're willing to relocate. Justification for including this information will be reviewed later in the book.

INTERESTS should include competitive first (golf, baseball), then noncompetitive activities (fishing, travel, gardening, etc.).

Most people whom I've counseled over the years have taken between one and two weeks to complete the homework assignment. If you have good documentation, you can usually complete the assignment within one week. Poor or nonexistent documentation will take you longer because you then have to get access to people with whom you used to work. Talk with people in both work and volunteer environments.

Chapter 8

HOW DO I ANALYZE MY RESUME?

You start with the market—*not* with you. What does it want that you'd be happy to sell it?

I did a presentation at a large church in Trenton, N.J., and one of the participants, John, an unemployed vice president of advertising, came in for the free consultation. Though he wanted to work with me, because he was unemployed for over a year, he declined due to cost. Then three weeks later he called to say he wanted to move ahead with my program.

When we met to start the counseling process, I inquired where he got the money. He said he borrowed it from his ex-wife to whom he was paying alimony and child support. After working together for several weeks, I had an initial draft of the resume for John to edit and emailed it to him. When we next met to review the resume draft and job-search mechanics, I asked him if he showed the resume draft to his ex-wife. He said of course, but added an interesting comment. He said that his ex-wife responded to reading the resume draft by stating that in the 20-plus years she and John had been married, she never had a clear understanding of what he did for a living until she read the resume draft.

Bottom line: If you can't explain to the person you're living with what you do for a living, how will you be able to communicate your **value** to a prospective employer? As an aside: this circumstance appears in the motion picture, "Bonfire of the Vanities."

* * *

Before we start to construct the marketing resume, let's carefully analyze each component, explaining:

- What it consists of
- Why it is placed in this location

- What are its strengths and weaknesses
- Examples of each component, and
- Additional comments

* * *

Below is **page one** of a typical marketing resume.

MICHAEL R. SMITH
3 Elm Street
Bellevue, New York 14211
716-201-1117 mrsmith@gmail.com

SUMMARY OF QUALIFICATIONS

Resourceful, analytical and responsive IT APPLICATION SUPPORT / INFRASTRUCTURE MANAGER with a proven history of success. Innovative and persistent problem solver who thrives on challenges, excels under pressure and gets the job done. Pragmatic, versatile and dedicated team builder who possesses strong interpersonal and good communication skills. Strong, hands-on leader and motivator, organized and thorough planner, and win/win negotiator dealing effectively across all levels of the company. Accustomed to a fast pace and multiple projects, fulfills priorities and balances competing agendas while consistently providing value-added advice to management, enabling them to achieve their strategic objectives.

Areas of Expertise

IT Project Management, including manpower estimation, time and action calendar preparation, cost estimates, talent evaluation and cross functional team building, status monitoring and reporting, change control, documentation, coordination and transition implementation planning, Sarbanes-Oxley control design and implementation.

Application Systems Support, including capacity and hardware planning, production migration, selecting appropriate technologies, insuring against application obsolescence via version/release management, process design and documentation, management and end user communication /notification, setting and managing expectations, data integrity and security, systems control and

127

troubleshooting, managing service levels and operational stability; managing service levels and operational stability.

Implementation Management, including developing release management strategy for individual systems, release approval-signoff, coordination and communication, identifying and prioritizing software release contents across multiple products/services, issue resolution, cross-functional team coordination and notification.

End-User Support, including vendor and tool selection, support team design, implementation, and metrics; knowledge base development, cross training, primary user contact, account creation; monitoring, design and implementation, support/helpdesk design and implementation, end-user communication and support strategies.

BUSINESS EXPERIENCE

2005 UPSTATE FINANCIAL, Buffalo, New York, a major financial services corporation
to   providing business loans and leases to small- and middle-market companies nationwide.
Present
   Production Support Database Administrator – 2010 to Present.

Responsible for availability of systems, verified backups, and creation of user accounts. Also responsible for resolving tier 1 and 2 SQL Database issues. Reported to Global Database Manager

- To support existing platform for client business unit after migration from unsupported UNIX platform, conceived, developed and implemented a comprehensive plan to upgrade Sybase 12.51 to 64 bit version. **Result**: implementation and testing completed through user acceptance testing (UAT).

   Production Support Manager – 2005 to 2009.

Responsible for day-to-day and long-term goal management of production support department. The department consisted of a technical team and help desk for the entire corporation. The department supported more than 875 global business users and $12 billion in assets. Managed 7 professionals and reported to Service Systems Manager.

* * *

Now that you've had an opportunity to study the first page of the marketing resume, let's take a closer look together.

MICHAEL R. SMITH

3 Elm Street

Bellevue, New York 14211

716-201-1117 mrsmith@gmail.com

This is a typical resume opening and provides all necessary contact information. Use the telephone number that is easiest for the caller to reach you; either home or cell. Some people provide both. Always include full address. Omitting your street address and instead using your LinkedIn address doesn't allow the reader to determine if you require a relocation. Include any professional designations after your name, i.e., CPA, RN, PE, MBA. It is acceptable to use only two lines instead of four.

MICHAEL R. SMITH   3 Elm Street

Bellevue, New York 14211   716-201-1117

* * *

SUMMARY OF QUALIFICATIONS

Use this statement to tell the reader to put the 10 seconds they will give your resume into the summary, and by inference, you'll answer the three key questions he wants to know:

1. What type of candidate am I holding? ("handle" to focus the reader)
2. What type of person are you? What's your management style?
3. What skill set / area of expertise am I buying?

Answering these questions will encourage your reader to go beyond the 10 seconds and read the full resume document, or at least, all of the first page and part of the second page.

* * *

"Resourceful, analytical and responsive IT APPLICATION SUPPORT / INFRASTRUCTURE MANAGER with a proven history of success. Innovative and persistent problem solver who thrives on challenges, excels under pressure and gets the job done. Pragmatic, versatile and dedicated team builder who possesses strong interpersonal and good communication skills. Strong, hands-on leader and motivator, organized and thorough planner, and win/win negotiator dealing effectively across all levels of the company. Accustomed to a fast pace and multiple projects, fulfills priorities and balances competing agendas while consistently providing value added advice to management, enabling them to achieve their strategic objectives."

This paragraph has two main objectives: First, to focus your reader by immediately stating what he's holding: an IT APPLICATION SUPPORT / INFRASTRUCTURE MANAGER. Since there is no way the reader can verify any of the information in this paragraph, he will immediately skip and proceed to the second paragraph: the areas of expertise. Because the first paragraph answers the questions below, it is vital that the information be based on 360° feedback from people with whom you've worked (peers, bosses, subordinates, vendors, clients or customers). When the reader *returns* to this paragraph, the second objective is to answer important personality/management style issues, including:

- Do I like you?
- Will you fit with my management team?
- Do you have the qualities to do the job?
- How do you handle pressure?
- Do you follow through?
- How do you characterize your interpersonal and communication skills?
- What is your management style?
- Are you organized?
- What is your negotiation style?
- How do you function in an organization?
- What type of work environment are you used to?
- How do you deal with competing agendas?

130

And most important, what is your personal **misson statement**. In other words, if hired, how do you function daily?

To make an informed hiring decision, organizations require this information from job candidates. Winning resumes provide this type of data.

If the recruiter calls you after reading your marketing resume, including this opening paragraph, she or he must hear on the phone what she or he read on the resume. If a disconnect occurs, the recruiter will discard your resume without calling you in for an interview.

If, however, during the phone call you match what is in the first paragraph, the recruiter's comfort level will go up, and you will have a better chance of getting the interview. When you take the interview, and again match the description on your resume, the recruiter's comfort level will be reinforced a second time, and this gives you an important competitive advantage.

When selecting a new position, most people in job search are looking for a good fit: the same objective desired by the hiring person. Thus, job search is really another form of courtship! Since there is no way to determine what the hiring manager is like as a personality, the best approach is for you to go first and describe what you're like as a personality on the job. If the hiring manager doesn't like your description, you won't get the interview. But if you're asked to schedule an interview, what has the hiring manager told you? Yes, he or she likes what was read, and thinks that you can be a good fit.

You can only achieve this type of result, however, by using 360°feedback from co-workers. Without it, all you will achieve is a disconnect, and a lack of interviews … much like you're currently experiencing, because the resume you're using fails to describe in detail your management style and personality.

* * *

Areas of Expertise

IT Project Management, including manpower estimation, time and action calendar preparation, cost estimates, talent evaluation and cross functional team building, status monitoring and reporting, change control, documentation, coordination and transition implementation planning, Sarbanes-Oxley control design and implementation.

Application Systems Support, including capacity and hardware planning, production migration, selecting appropriate technologies, insuring against application obsolescence via version/release management, process design and documentation, management and end user communication /notification, setting and managing expectations, data integrity and security, systems control and troubleshooting, managing service levels and operational stability; managing service levels and operational stability.

Implementation Management, including developing release management strategy for individual systems, release approval-signoff, coordination and communication, identifying and prioritizing software release contents across multiple products/services, issue resolution, cross-functional team coordination and notification.

End-User Support, including vendor and tool selection, support team design, implementation, and metrics; knowledge base development, cross training, primary user contact, account creation; monitoring, design and implementation, support/helpdesk design and implementation, end-user communication and support strategies.

The "Areas of Expertise" section of the marketing resume answers the critical question: Can you do the job technically? Since the first paragraph describing your personality is not believable, the reader will stop after the first sentence and jump to the expertise. This resume section creates credibility with the reader, because the skills explained are in **process** terms that match the processes used in the reader's organization. **This is a very important point**.

** Process is the first transferable skill used in the marketing resume, and is the foundation for the entire document's credibility.

Here is what one of my clients told me a leading international executive recruiting firm had said about his resume:

"Egon Zehnder also provided extremely positive feedback on the information content of the resume."

If you read any of the areas of expertise above, you will notice that the definition for each of the topics (I call them headings) is in the proper sequence, and uses the proper terminology / jargon related to the topic. Writing in this way says to the reader that you **have been there and done that!**

You're experienced, require little or no training, and can provide immediate productivity. In a nutshell, you represent a better "buy."

This conclusion encourages the recruiter to continue reading beyond the usual 10 seconds. After reviewing the entire resume, the recruiter returns to the first paragraph and reads it fully for the first time. Again, he or she won't believe what you've written about yourself. But he or she has a simple way to verify what you wrote. Since you have demonstrated that you can do the job technically, they call you on the phone and expect you to match the resume description. You will if the summary is based on 360° feedback from co-workers. Without 360° feedback, the opening paragraph is not believable.

Another important quality of the summary of qualifications is its flexibility. If you use two headings, as in this IT example, it will allow you to easily create **four versions of your marketing resume.** Do this by:

- First rearranging the heading into four different groupings:

    a. IT APPLICATION SUPPORT / INFRASTRUCTURE MANAGER
    b. INFRASTRUCTURE MANAGER /IT APPLICATION SUPPORT
    c. INFRASTRUCTURE MANAGER
    d. IT APPLICATION SUPPORT MANAGER

- Then rearrange your accomplishments in the PAR format to match the new heading arrangement.

In this way, the marketing resume will provide you with four versions of the same information, and will allow you to go after several different positions at the same time. Also, it allows you to send out a lot of resumes quickly, because there is no rewriting, only rearranging.

Important note: The marketing resume is *not* constructed for any particular position. Instead, it says to the recruiter and hiring manager:

1. Here is the expertise that I can bring to your organization.
2. These are the type of problems / issues that I have experience solving.
3. This is what I'm like as a personality, and this is my management style.

Where, Mr./Ms. Executive, do you think you could use me?

Important point: Don't state what position you're applying for. Instead, let the reader first understand the skills you possess, your management style, what you're like as a personality, and the type of problems / issues you have solved. This understanding will allow managers and executives to make a more informed "buying" decision.

* * *

BUSINESS EXPERIENCE

You can characterize your work experience in several ways. Most frequently, people will use the term "Professional Experience." Other terms frequently used include: Professional History, Work Experience, Experience, Work, or not call it by any term at all.

The best term to use is Business Experience, because it tells your reader at the outset that you think in business terms, not technical terms. Besides, the hiring manager doesn't want you to compete in technical terms anyway.

* * *

2005 to Present   UPSTATE FINANCIAL, Buffalo, New York, a major financial services corporation providing business loans and leases to small- and middle-market companies nationwide.

Production Support Database Administrator – 2010 to Present.

Responsible for availability of systems, verified backups, and creation of user accounts. Also responsible for resolving tier 1 and 2 SQL Database issues. Reported to Global Database Manager

- To support existing platform for client business unit after migration from unsupported UNIX platform, conceived, developed and implemented a comprehensive plan to upgrade Sybase 12.51 to 64 bit version. **Result**: implementation and testing completed through user acceptance testing (UAT).

Production Support Manager – 2005 to 2009.

Responsible for day-to-day and long-term goal management of production support department. The department consisted of a technical team and help desk for the entire corporation. The department supported more than 875 global business users and $12 billion in assets. Managed 7 professionals and reported to Service Systems Manager.

In describing the employer, I use two types of layouts. The above layout is used when the candidate has more than one job title with the employer. In this configuration, the company name comes first, in all capitals but not bold. Since **we're promoting the candidate, not the employer**, bolding is reserved for **job titles**. Use full years, not month and year. This allows you to hide breaks in employment more easily. Also note that total employment dates are in the margin on the left, and individual job dates follow the job title. If all the dates were either in the left or right margin, the impression would be that you're a job hopper when, in fact, you're not. Avoid this impression at all cost.

* * *

The second layout configuration used in the marketing resume involves those situations where the candidate has only one job title. Example:

2005
to
2010
    Acting Controller/Senior Accountant, STROWE MANUFACTURING LLC, Albany, NY, a medium-size fabricator of retail display fixtures for the pharmaceutical industry with sales of $150 million and 1,400 employees.

Prepared P&L statements for four divisions and related footnotes. Developed reporting procedures, assisted in the implementation of new accounting standards, and managed the marketing budget. Matrix- managed two professionals and reported to controller. During the controller's leave of absence, appointed acting controller, managed 6 employees and reported to the CFO.

In this example, the candidate is a senior accountant; since his boss is out on leave, he was named acting controller. In this situation, the candidate has only one permanent job title, senior accountant, and an acting title. Since the acting title "sells" better, always take credit for the work that you do and lead off with the more senior title. Placing the job title and company information on the same line saves space in the resume and is recommended. Justify this arrangement during the interview by saying, "Acting controller is my functional title while senior accountant is my payroll title."

* * *

The next part of the marketing resume is the accomplishments, and should be described using the PAR method. Here are some examples from five job categories:

IT: • To improve workforce effectiveness, consulted with manager in the conception, advocacy, design, and implementation of an automated physical inventory system, replacing manual paper system with automated real-time entry and verification using handheld scanner devices. **Result**: reduced the number and duration of wall-to-wall inventories from two annual, seven-day inventories of 13,000 to 14,000 pallets, during plant shutdowns, to one annual inventory completed in four days. *(J.Salter)*

HR: • To reduce loss of key resources during transformation, designed and implemented a retention program which included mentoring, career development, participation in special projects, and bimonthly management status update. **Result**: no turnover of key resources. *(S. Chang)*

Accounting: • To handle a greater volume of payroll issues and remain in both federal and state compliance, interfaced with payroll service and identified software product to address our processing concerns. Negotiated ongoing service agreement. Trained staff. **Result**: achieved multi-user, multi-source system; expanded system to add wage garnishment module and report writer module. *(Name?)*

Internet: • To create a new presence in the sports supplement category, created a dedicated and innovative website that showcased the product line and educated consumers about natural supplements. **Result**: generated sense of urgency among customers and product consistently sold out during the first three months after launch. *(Trish)*

Sales: • To reverse declining market share with major customer, established open communications, instituted regular stewardship meeting around servicing and business project identification. Became trusted business advisor to three BU heads. Generated proposals for video conferencing, instant messaging and IT infrastructure. **Result**: client's account management satisfaction rating increased 50%; sold additional services increasing wallet share by 25% and generated $5 million per year for 5 years. *(Weijer)*

Notice that each accomplishment begins with the statement of a problem or issue. Leading off with a problem is the **second transferable skill**, and allows your reader to possibly conclude that your experience matches their needs. If so, you've answered one of the three issues needed to get hired:

1. Have you solved our type of problems?
2. Can you do the job technically?
3. Will you fit with our management team?

Note: If you use the three elements of the PAR format, but don't begin with the Problem, you resume will look like everyone else's. Avoid this mistake.

The PAR method will be discussed in great detail in Chapter 9. For now, you only need to know the definition of the PAR format.

Problem: Should be universal or generic
Action: Tell *what* you did, not how (i.e., no free consulting)
Result: Use numbers, percentages, time or testimonials

* * *

Resume development continues using an inverse chronological format and by repeating either of the two types of layouts:

More than one job title with an employer:

Employer defined; total dates in left margin
Current job title-dates after title; responsibilities defined
Accomplishments described using PAR method

Only one job title with an employer:

> Current job title, employer defined; total dates in left margin
> Responsibilities defined
> Accomplishments described using PAR

The last 15 years of your work history needs to be covered in detail. Your prior work history can be covered in a few sentences, but the time frame must be explained. Remember, no surprises! If your detailed work history has not convinced the reader to bring you in for an interview, nothing you say about your previous experience will change his mind. So keep this section short.

If your most recent position contributes little to the experience you're trying to "sell" a future employer, don't give it a lot of space on the first page of your resume. Instead, limit it to only one or two lines. In a sense, this tells the recruiter why you're looking for a new position.

* * *

PAGE TWO of the marketing resume (model)

The remainder of the marketing resume sample represents examples taken from several different clients' resumes.

* * *

1993
to
1995

UNITED STATES ARMY.

Human Resources Manager/Operations Manager/Training Director - First Sergeant, Ft. Hood, TX, and Friedberg, Germany – 1993 to 1995.

Supervised 63 employees, including 4 team leaders; lead change agent, organizational development, change management, project management and program development.

- To achieve budgetary savings during a time of reduced allowances, developed and implemented a unique and innovative plan for alternative training area and mode of transportation. **Result**: reduced transportation costs from more than $1500 to less than $50 per training event saving $100,000 and eliminated the cost for required training areas ($93,000).

EDUCATION

B.S., Business Administration / Accounting, RUTGERS UNIVERSITY, 1985. International Finance, UNIVERSITY OF NEW HAVEN, currently enrolled in MBA program. Specialized training in Personnel Management, COBRA, International Assignments, and Immigration and Naturalization Law.

LANGUAGES Read, write and speak Spanish fluently; working knowledge of French.

CERTIFICATION & AWARDS CPA, Maryland, 1997. Completed Six Sigma Green Belt training. AT&T Shackleton Award.

AFFILIATIONS IEEE, ASTD, CFA Institute. NYSSA.

PERSONAL DATA

Married, one child; excellent health. Willing to travel and open to relocation.

INTERESTS

Golf, soccer, debating, volunteering at church activities, theater and art museums.

* * *

Military experience is valuable, and always demonstrates a number of qualities in the candidate, including team work and leadership experience. Treat military experience the same as any other work experience, and record it on the resume the same way. Though the "employer," U.S. Army, doesn't need to be defined, the job title, location, responsibility and accomplishments should be explained in the same manner as the rest of the marketing resume.

Always provide your date of graduation. The marketing resume is a full disclosure / no surprises document. If someone wants to discriminate against you, let him or her. You don't want to work for them anyway. Age is not the issue. **The only issue in job search is the monkeys on the hiring executives' back and the value you bring to a new employer**.

Recent graduates can include their grade-point average if it works to their advantage. Also, recent graduates should discuss any leadership positions they had, and awards received. Some young clients from top-tier colleges position their education at the top of the resume after their Areas of Expertise.

* * *

The ability to speak a foreign language even partially is very valuable, and can be the difference between landing the job or being the bridesmaid. If you are fluent in a foreign language, indicate it at the very top of your resume, like so:

"Resourceful, analytical and responsive Spanish-speaking IT APPLICATION SUPPORT / INFRASTRUCTURE MANAGER with a proven history of success.

Many people, especially Information Technology candidates, like to put their computer languages, operating systems and applications under the languages heading on their resume. Rather than take up valuable resume space, consider this strategy: create a Keyword Summary and store it in white ink as an extra page in your resume. That way the HR departments HRIS optical scanner will flag your resume but print out your document with a blank last page. Neat trick. Try it. It works some of the time. Here's an example that uses every term that could possibly relate to the job candidate's background and experience.

Keyword Summary

Acceptance, Analysis, Captivate, classroom, compliance, computer, continuity, data collection, demonstrations, development, disaster, distributed, documentation, Documentation, End-user support, HTML, HTML Help, information, integration, Internet, Intranet, LAN/WAN, lifecycle, Mainframe, management, manuals, Marketing, MS Office, PC, process, product, program, project, quality, quality assurance, regression, requirements, RoboHelp, software, specifications, support, system, Systems Analyst, technical writing, training materials, technology, testing, tools, training, vendor, videoconferencing, web

* * *

List all your certifications and awards, even if they have expired.

CPA, New Jersey 1999–2005. New York State, current.
Series 7 Certification, 2001–2013.
Series 63 (expired).

* * *

List all your professional affiliations first, then other nonprofessional affiliations. You can mention civic, political and religious affiliations, but keep them general; don't mention specific political party or religious affiliation. Do mention any leadership roles that you held.

* * *

Many people object to including marital status. I recommend its inclusion for reasons of full disclosure and to show stability. There are only two statuses to use: single or married. Don't tell the reader that your head is all messed up by stating that you're separated or divorced.

Include your health, and state any issue or disability that is obvious or will show up in a physical examination.

Example: issue: cold, sweaty hands. Explanation: poor circulation in my right hand.

If you're willing to travel and or relocate, tell your reader. In many situations, the ability to relocate or not can be a deal breaker.

* * *

Another example of INTERESTS:

Golf, soccer, debating, coaching Little League baseball, volunteering at church activities, theater and art museums.

You should cover competitive interests first and then non-competitive interests. If you're applying for a position that requires interpersonal skills, your interests should not tell people that you're basically a loner. Coaching youth sports alerts the reader that you know how to motivate without using money. It sells well, so use it if you have the experience.

CHAPTER 9

VALID TRANSFERABLE SKILLS WILL BEAT THE COMPETITION!

Learn how to identify and apply them in new ways.

Some years ago, I counseled a customer service manager from the technology group of a large bank supporting the brokerage industry. Some weeks after working with him to complete his resume and counseling, I noticed an ad in *The Wall Street Journal* for a product manager at a small software-development firm serving large financial institutions. The requirements in the ad directly matched my client's background and experience. I answered the ad using a "blind" version of his resume, one that did not identify the person or his employer by name. He got the interview, then another, and subsequently was hired into the position, despite the fact that the ad said "MBA preferred." My client had no MBA, no college degree, and only 50 credits toward an associate's degree that requires 60 credits.

What's going on here? How can a company advertise for an MBA and wind up hiring a candidate who only has 50 credits and no degree? I didn't have an answer to this question until a few years later, when I was reading an article in *Crain's New York Business* entitled "Audacity, Charisma Boost Matchmaker" by Pamela Bayless. I came across this statement in the article where the matchmaker is explaining how she achieves her successful matches. She said: "People know what they want, but not what they need," she says. "When we give them what they need, they forget what they want."

The explanation why my candidate was hired turned out to be simple. The company knew what it wanted. It was contained in the want ad, but did not convey what the company needed. My candidate's resume represented what the company needed—experience outlined in PAR format, skills in process terms, and chemistry/**fit**. The company then forgot that it wanted an MBA.

* * *

My argument remains true: You don't need a great education or certification. What you need is **presentation**—in your resume and the interview.

Everyone Has Transferable Skills

The need to effectively change industries has become ever more necessary in the past few years, due to the financial crisis and the downsizing of key industries like publishing, financial, pharmaceutical and education, to name a few.

The dean of American management consulting, Peter Drucker, made the following interesting observation:

"Most business issues were generic issues—repetitions of familiar problems cloaked in the guise of uniqueness."

Most business issues or problems are basically the same, regardless of industry. You probably know this truth. When you last changed jobs and went to work for a new employer, the business issues you became involved in were basically similar to those you handled at previous employers.

What You Don't Need:

- more education
- more certifications
- more experience

What You Do Need:

- **presentation** based on transferable skills!

If you identify your transferable skills and then communicate them properly, you can successfully transfer to other industries without taking a pay cut. In many cases, you can increase compensation. This point is made clear in the discussion that opened this chapter.

What You're Up Against

In reality, recruiters and hiring managers are very skeptical, because of so many lies in resumes. Thus, you need to start your accomplishments with the problem or issue.

In 1992, the newspaper *USA Today* ran a graph showing that 36 percent of information in resumes was either lies or distortions. Ten years later, the Government Accounting Office (GAO) did a research study regarding resumes and found that 38 percent of the information was either lies or distortions as well. In 2004, ADP published the results of a study showing how widespread resume padding still is. ADP said it based its findings on 2.6 million background verifications it performed during one year only. It found that 44 percent of employment records showed a difference between information the applicant provided and what a past employer reported.

> **Bottom line**: The readers of your resume won't believe your accomplishment results because they're already very skeptical of what is written in resumes, and you're an unknown. Why should they believe anything you say about yourself? This, however, will not be the case if you add a transferable skill, *the problem*, to your accomplishments.

So what is believable to external recruiters, HR recruiters, hiring managers and executives?

Merriam-Webster's Collegiate Dictionary defines "transferable" as a verb meaning "to move to a different place, region or situation."

Outplacement services use such terms as seasoned, hard-working, adaptable, analytical, conscientious, or diplomatic. All these terms, however, are qualities, not transferable skills.

What is a transferable skill? Basically, it is a skill that can be applied across numerous industries and job levels.

A transferable skill is an ability that is *self-evident* to the reader or listener, and *requires no further verification*. I have found that there are only two transferable skills: **process** (correct sequence and terminology) and **problems** (issue, need, situation, opportunity, circumstance).

Take the term **sales**. What does the reader know about the candidate's understanding of this term? Really, he or she knows very little; only that *you* know the term. Our job search model has three legs that satisfy the basis of *all* hiring decisions... and two of these legs will allow you to introduce your *transferable skills*. Without emphasizing transferable skills, candidates are limiting themselves to their present industry. Yet your career future probably lies in a different industry. Don't unnecessarily dead-end your career. Prevent this common resume practice by emphasizing *your* transferable skills.

Much talk and many articles stress the importance of demonstrating transferable skills when developing your job-search marketing materials. Few articles, however, discuss how to document your work history in ways that *demonstrate* transferable skills.
Yet, if you define your transferable skills and can communicate them properly, you can successfully transfer to other industries without taking a pay cut. In many cases you could increase compensation. Let me explain.

A transferable skill is one where the reader of your resume can recognize it, compare it against something he or she personally encountered, recognize it matches with their background and experience, and conclude that the resume writer has "been there and done that." Basically, it is a skill that can be applied across numerous industries and job levels. A good example is sales.

Most business issues or problems are basically the same regardless of industry. Think for a moment. When you last changed jobs and went to work for a new employer, the business issues you became involved with were basically similar to those you handled at your previous employer. For example, when I counsel clients with a financial background, I always recommend starting their new job by going after the "low hanging fruit," such as accounts receivable (a basic financial function), to achieve a quick, cost-effective impact.

Take the example of sales, which is part of the list above. This is a good example, because most people have a basic understanding of sales. What if you use the term "sales" in your resume without explaining what you mean by it? The reader will conclude very little from the use of this term. What if, however, your resume said: "Sales, including prospecting (warm and cold calling), scheduling appointments with decision-makers, executive presentation and follow-up, closing, key account management, time and territory management, and continuous customer relations"?

What would a recruiter or hiring manager conclude?

Probably that you know sales, because you have explained the same steps in the sales process that is used universally. In other words: you *have* been there and done that. This creates credibility with your readers. They don't have to make assumptions or jump to conclusions. You provided the evidence.

The key to writing your skills in transferable language is to make sure that you describe *all* the basic elements of a particular skill in the proper sequence, and with the proper jargon or terminology. In other words, describe your understanding of the **process**, whether it's the sales process, project management process, or curriculum design process. To help you think in process terms, the outline below describes the sequential steps necessary to successfully solve any problem. People with training or experience in project management are familiar with the outline.

How are Problems Solved?

1. **Gather data**—historical review, observation, interviewing or questionnaire
2. **Analyze the data**
3. **Develop action plan**
4. **Gather resources**
    a. Consensus building
    b. Negotiating approvals
5. **Implementation**
6. **Documentation**
7. **Evaluation and reporting**

Skill Set Example

Let's try writing a classic area of expertise: project management.

Below are four definition examples of the skill set called project management. Based on your experience, cut and paste to create a definition that reflects your experience completing projects. Remember, you only need to describe the basic elements of the process. Breaking down each element in the definition into sub-elements only lengthens the definition without achieving additional value. It also makes you come across as too wordy.

Example 1: **Project Management**, from project definition with stakeholders through deployment and closeout, including cost and risk analysis, work breakdown structures, scheduling and resource management, budgeting, communications planning, tracking and forecasting, contract compliance, change management, quality control, documentation and performance analysis, and reporting.

Example 2: **Program/Project Management**, from initiation to closeout, including situation analysis, objectives definition and alignment with program/business objectives, negotiating stakeholder approval, scope and risk management (identification, quantification, response development and control); contractor selection; progress tracking (input to risk assessment, along with business impact, scope/complexity and resources), *ad hoc* issue resolution; senior management reporting; and development of lessons learned.

Example 3: **Cross-Functional Project Management**: Gathering business requirements from stakeholders to deployment and maintenance, including creating and presenting work breakdown structures and negotiating effective communication methods, project planning and risk identification, project execution, cost performance tracking, documentation, post-mortem analysis, and executive reporting.

Example 4: **Project Management**, from project definition with stakeholders through deployment to closeout, including: Customer relationship building, managing cross-functional teams, cost and risk analysis, work breakdown structures, scheduling and resource management, budgeting, communications planning, tracking and forecasting, contract compliance, change management, quality control, documentation, performance analysis, issue resolution, and reporting to senior management.

Work Area:

_____

_____

_____

Now review carefully what you've written. Does your definition of the project management skill set satisfy these conditions?

1. Comprehensive—covers the basic elements or steps in the process,
2. Elements are in the correct sequence, and
3. Proper, recognized / agreed jargon or terminology is used

Here is our example:

Project Management, from gathering business requirements from stakeholders to deployment and maintenance, including creating and presenting work breakdown structures and negotiating effective communication methods, project planning and risk identification, project execution, cost performance tracking, documentation and post-mortem analysis, and executive reporting.

Process Examples:

If you compare the two examples for sales, you can see the advantage of the longer approach. It confirms that "you've been there and done that."

Sales *(this short statement on the top of a typical job candidate's resume is how most people attempt to demonstrate their skill set; it clearly fails to demonstrate anything to the hiring audience)*

Versus:

Sales, including telephone prospecting, scheduling appointments with decision-makers, defining customer needs, executive presentations and follow-up, contract negotiations, closing, key account management, time and territory management, and customer relations.

Problem Examples:

- To capture market share from competition, applied consultative sales approach to both new and existing customers. **Result**: overall sales increased 58% in 3 years, from $1.9 million to $3.0 million. This far outpaced the construction market index, which averaged 14% growth annually.

- To control expenses at 42 locations, managed the M3 Accounts Payable System and closely monitored the charge-back procedure. Established team of hotel controllers, along with an Internet-based A/P system. **Result**: reduced A/R from more than 45 days to 15-20 days, achieving a significant increase in cash flow.

Communicating Your Transferable Skills

Using transferable skills will give you an important competitive edge. Your competition doesn't use this method to describe their experience. Here's proof:

The New Jersey state trade association for the Council of Logistics Management provided a service to unemployed members by reproducing their resumes, organizing them into binders, and distributing these binders to major corporations throughout the state. Through a client, I obtained a copy of the binder and analyzed its 210 resumes. Here are the results:

Analysis Factors	#	%
Right-justified	118	56
Personality Characteristics	5	2
Different Font Styles	49	23
PAR Paragraphs	0	0
Areas of Expertise	20	9.5
Military Experience	39	18.5
Master's Degree	70	33

From this analysis, I concluded that most people prepare their resumes incorrectly. No one is talking about the hiring manager's problems (PAR), only 2 percent provide personality characteristics, and yet "fit" is 90 percent of the basis for a hiring decision. Finally, only 9.5 percent of the resumes provided a skill set (Areas of Expertise). Yet this is the most important issue to "hook" the reader at the very beginning of your resume.

* * *

Conclusion: If you answer the three key issues in your resume, you will out-market a majority of your competition in any job for which you apply. The competition may be technically more qualified than you, but you would be perceived as the better candidate!

When presenting your experience in a resume or during an interview, it is important to concentrate on **executing the basics**. Don't talk about issues that you were particularly proud of, which may fail to match the hiring executive's needs. Rather, talk about the issues that the *interviewer* is concerned about; the problems on the hiring executive's back. How to determine the hiring executive's needs is covered in Chapter 10(job-search mechanics).

Most job seekers use a resume format that fails to meet the hiring executive's needs. Instead, they use the HR format that fails to answer the three questions that form the basis of <u>all decisions to hire</u>.

1. Can you do the job technically?
2. Have you solved the same types of problems as the hiring executive?
3. Will you fit with the hiring executive's management team? Does he or she like you more than the other candidates?

If you answer these questions on your resume, you're doing the recruiter's job. You're creating an executive recruiter's resume and encouraging him or her to present your credentials to employers. You've made it easy for the recruiter to "sell" you.

Another key point: Don't prepare your resume for a specific job or title. By writing your resume for a specific job, you're actually limiting the reader's ability to consider you for more than a single position. A better approach is to draft a resume document that encourages hiring executives to consider you for multiple positions. Concentrating on the two transferable skills will allow you to achieve this objective.

Achieve this objective by **competing in business terms, *not* technical terms**. To expand your job-search options, construct your resume from a *business* perspective. Always address the hiring executive's needs, by solving issues, making or saving money, time and labor; also talk about solving both short- and long-term issues.

Quiz: Identify the correct answer.

Executives and recruiters are your principal audiences. ___T ___F

Your resume is critical in obtaining interviews. ___T ___F

What is the best way to compete? ___ in business terms ___in technical terms

The resume is the basis of a person's confidence level. ___T ___F

What's the best way to compete in a tough job market? ___get an MBA ___ presentation ___ obtain more certifications

If the interviewer can't "sell" you to their boss, he/she won't present you to their boss.
____ T ____ F

Select the **three key factors** in most hiring decisions:

____ Do you have a college education?

____ Does your personality fit with the rest of the department?

____ Are you affordable and competitively priced?

____ Do you have experience solving the hiring executive's problems?

____ Are you younger than 40?

____ In a new job, concentrate on executing the basics.

____ Most business issues are generic issues.

____ Are you a strategic thinker?

____ Can you commit to more than a two-year contract?

____ Did you work for our major competitor?

____ Can you do the job technically?

____ Did your resume highlight transferable skills?

RESUME CONTENT: Financial Example

To create a resume that reflects a business orientation, on what should you concentrate, and what should you ignore?

To begin, don't emphasize the usual personal testimony issues (e.g., what you're most proud of), unless it corresponds with hiring executive's needs. Instead, review in your resume those issues that "sell" best with the hiring audience ("C-suite" executives, division and department managers, and executive/employment recruiters). Let's apply this approach to a financial executive. Key fundamental issues involved in most financial positions:

- Accurate and timely financial reporting
- Cash and working capital management
- Accounting-department discipline
- Mergers and acquisitions (in good times)
- Expense control (in bad times)

Only use topics like Sarbanes-Oxley and SEC reporting as filler in the resume.

Communicating Your Value—Areas of Expertise / Skill Set

You need to explain in detail what **skill set** the reader of your resume is buying. This is the easiest way to create credibility, because it demonstrates transferable skills and can be accomplished within 10 seconds.

Example: Stating that you're skilled in **sales** says nothing to your reader. If, however, you explain in process terms what you mean, your reader can identify with the process, because it's similar to the sales process they use. Conclusion: You've "been there and done that."
>   a. Failing to communicate your skills: • sales
>   b. Proving your credibility and you can do the job:
>   **Sales**, including prospecting (warm calling and cold calling), scheduling appointments with decision-makers, executive presentations, contract negotiations, closing, key account management, time and territory management, and continuous customer service.

By explaining each of your skills/areas of expertise in process terms, you encourage recruiters to compare your understanding of a particular skill with their own understanding. If your explanation is in the proper sequence, and uses the appropriate industry jargon/terminology, you've successfully demonstrated "you've been there and done that" and are a very credible candidate that should be hired.

You will:

- come up to speed quickly,
- require little or no training,
- take on additional responsibilities,
- represent less risk, and
- be a better hire.

Answer to **Quiz**:

- Quiz – Identify the correct answer
  1. T 2. T 3. in business terms 4. T 5. presentation 6. T 7. Does your personality fit? Do you have experience solving similar problems? Can you do the job technically?

Chapter 10

STRENGTHEN THE MECHANICS OF YOUR JOB SEARCH
Taking the Show on the Road

Lack of Industry Experience / Universal, Rather Than a Specific Resume

Story

At a talk I gave in New Canaan, Connecticut, I met the director of finance for a major international food corporation. He had just completed six months with a large outplacement firm, without success.

Since many of my concepts resonated with his business experience, he decided to accept my offer for a free consultation. Liking what he heard, and impressed with the sample marketing resume and support materials, he decided to sign up and work with me. Through his connections at his employer, he was able to get the company to pay a second outplacement fee.

8/01:	Free consultation.
8/22:	Review homework; start counseling process
9/04:	Three- to five-hour counseling session to create marketing resume. Client returned home to complete two additional assignments: creating an elevator- and two-minute pitch, and a two-page networking handout.
10/10:	Final meeting; review all aspects of job search.

During our final counseling session, while reviewing how best to work with executive recruiters, I suggested my client do a major mailing to both domestic and international recruiters.

He was contacted by Egon Zehnder, a leading international executive search firm. My client commented to me: "They also provided extremely positive feedback on the information content of the resume." Although all of my client's experience was in consumer-package goods corporations, the recruiter then arranged for my client to interview with two companies:

1. Crane Corporation, a $2.5 billion manufacturer of high-tech industrial valves, and
2. Biogen Idec, a $1.5 billion biotech firm in Boston, and also Bern, Switzerland.

In the case of Biogen, 300 resumes were screened and four candidates were invited in for the initial interview. All interviewees had strong credentials in accounting, and had managed a finance department outside of the United States. Two people were invited back for the second round of interviews.

Using six **additional closing documents**, including one called "Get the job by doing the job," my client was hired by the biotech firm, despite his total lack of **any** industry experience.

Bottom line: Based on the strength of my client's resume, the recruiter and employer were willing to "think outside the box."

* * *

Being unconventional, I will be presenting the classic method of conducting a job search, and will leave Internet search to those individuals who enjoy competing against thousands of candidates (and who believe a 3 percent Internet placement rate is to their advantage). Instead, I will argue for using networking, external recruiters, professional trade journals, and writing directly to the hiring executive as the more effective way to generate interviews and land a good position that will advance your career.

JOB-SEARCH ACTIVITY SEQUENCE

Conventional wisdom holds that most people obtain their new jobs through networking. This is a myth promoted by the outplacement firms, because it maximizes their profits. My experience, and that of the *Recruiting & Search Report* of Panama City Beach, Florida, know that direct-mail approaches **and** networking are the most effective.

As a result, I recommend that you conduct your job search in the following sequence.

Step I: Do a thorough **remailing** using your new marketing resume to everyone who received your previous resume. This includes recruiters, networking contacts, ads if "open," people who interviewed you, names of persons in rejection letters, etc.

Step II: Conduct a major mailing to recruiters nationwide. If you have a strong international background, also do a major mailing to international recruiters. It is not unusual for a **recruiter** in Houston to be recruiting for M&M/Mars in Hackettstown, New Jersey. Remember, with the exception of your career coach, the recruiter is the only person who can make a buck off of you in the job-search process. Make it easy for them to help you! That is what the marketing resume approach is all about.

Step III: Write directly to employers for whom you want to work. This **direct mail** approach requires that you obtain proprietary mailing lists. For this, you will need to do a good piece of research on the Internet and at a good library. In addition, like working your personal contacts, you conduct your direct mail from "C" companies, to "B" companies, to "A" companies. Since you need to practice your interviewing and salary-negotiation skills, the best place to do this is with companies you may *not* want to work for—your "C" companies. Then move up to the "B" companies, and finally to the "A" (best) companies.

The most important issue in the direct-mail strategy is what to send to companies as your direct-mail "package." Does the first 10 seconds of your marketing letter or resume cover letter catch the reader's interest? If not, then your direct-mail campaign will yield few, if any, results.

Your direct-mail package will be the result of several choices, including:

Resume approach:

1. Marketing resume plus areas of expertise-based cover letter.
2. Marketing resume plus PAR-based cover letter.
3. Marketing resume plus rhetorical question / pitch cover letter.

Non-resume approach:

These are most useful if your resume mailings are being routed to the human resources department (gatekeepers), without evidence that the hiring executive (your target audience) ever saw your cover letter and resume.

4. PAR letter only (see *Wall Street Journal*'s NEBW article reprint in the Appendix).
5. Rhetorical question / pitch letter.
6. Areas of expertise-based letter.

In deciding, which approach to use, remember that the biggest prejudice in the job market is **lack of industry experience**. The best way to overcome this is by using a resume approach with the cover letter that repeats your *areas of expertise.*

Step IV: The fourth and final way to generate job leads is through **networking**. See my three-part article on value-added networking at the end of this chapter.

Step V: **Answering advertisements** in the newspapers, trade magazines or on the Internet. When answering ads, it is important to **come in at the end** of the HR department's resume-review process. This is what I call the "pizza box"; sometimes, a statement on the cover of the pizza box says:"You've Tried the Rest—Now Try the Best." Translated into job-search jargon: You've Seen the Rest—Now See the Best!

Continue to answer ads throughout your job search while following the steps above. Just be sure to follow the "pizza box" strategy.

Final point: Repeat mailings, using a different direct-mail strategy some weeks or months later, is recommended. Remember: You can never step into the same stream twice, because the stream is always changing, and so is the job market. One day when your potential employer receives your materials, they may have no opening or need. But the very next day, after a resignation, they may have a need for your skills and experience. Therefore, the only thing that counts in the job search is *action—continuous action!*

Getting Started

To implement this type of job-search strategy, you will require certain support materials.

Support Materials

1. Printing

I recommend you offset-print your resume only with a local printer; i.e., not a "Staples" type of organization. Recommended paper is Classic Laid / Natural White, using 11-point type size and Times New Roman font. Cover letter should also be on the same paper as your resume, but run off your home printer. Learning to use mail-merge will prove extremely valuable in your search, save you a lot of time, and make you more efficient.

2. Elevator Pitch

To be able to explain yourself succinctly during a telephone interview, in a networking meeting, or to answer the classic "Tell me about yourself" is extremely valuable. To help you achieve this objective, two examples are provided below. But first, what is an elevator pitch?

"An elevator pitch is a short, 15- to 30-second, 40- to 60-word sound bite that *memorably* introduces you. It spotlights your uniqueness by focusing on the benefits you provide, and is delivered effortlessly. It helps to begin a conversation and passes the "so what" test. If you can say "so what" after your elevator pitch, you're not selling a benefit to your listener. Remember, your elevator pitch isn't about you, it's about **how you add value**." From *Opening Doors with a Brilliant Elevator Speech,* by Jeffrey J. Mayer:

Example: Hi, my name is S.S., and for more than eight years in retail construction, I have consistently reduced dollar-per-square-foot construction costs through the streamlining of processes and implementation of value-added strategies.

Example: For more than 13 years, I have been solving major business-process issues at the senior level. I have done this in the areas of sales, finance and operations. My main expertise is in strategic and tactical planning, as well as productivity improvement.

Now try this *template* based on the above example. It is very effective, and is the single easiest way to strengthen your confidence.

For more than ___ years, I have been solving _____ issues at the _____ level. I have done this in the areas of _____, _____ and _____. My main expertise is in _____, _____ and _____.

3. Two-Minute Pitch

Nobody is going to listen to a job candidate give a two-minute pitch. So why bother to even prepare one? Surprisingly, it will come in handy for two very important situations. The first is to post the full pitch on the wall next to your home telephone, so when you get a call, usually from HR recruiters at inopportune times, you can refer to the pitch and come across as very professional. The second situation is to put the full pitch into a cover letter for recruiters or other audiences. See sample below.

Example of a Two-Minute Pitch:

For more than 13 years, I have been solving major business process issues at the senior level. I have done this in the areas of sales, finance and operations. My main expertise is in strategic and tactical planning, productivity improvement, business process re-design, and financial management and reporting.

As a regional finance director for a major food corporation—one of the most successful consumer-packaged goods companies in the world—I have developed a thorough understanding of managing the business process, including long-range strategic planning, short-term goal setting, and action planning, along with cost-control methodologies.

Among my accomplishments, I have:

- Created strategic visions and fact-based selling plans that successfully developed the business and increased market share in the Boston region from $135 million to $266 million, and from 28 percent to 49 percent in only five years.

- Strengthened supply-chain efficiency by facilitating a series of planning meetings between sales, operations and finance. Created jointly owned performance scorecard and rearranged job accountabilities.

- Prepared business analysis with specific recommendations that improved profit margin by 0.7 percent or $2.9 million annually.

- Implemented local coaching initiatives and tracking, reporting, and analysis tools that allowed us to beat aggressive cost targets by more than $635,000.

I am now looking for an opportunity where I can leverage my skills and experience in a larger role. I am particularly effective at developing and achieving a company's business plan.

Another **Pitch Example**:

For more than 17 years, I have been solving business development issues at the senior level. I have done this in the areas of industrial / commercial real estate, energy efficiency, and alternative fuels. My main expertise is in contract negotiations, technology introduction, and revenue-generation strategies.

I recently completed a consulting contract for Federal Business Centers, a premier New Jersey real estate developer and majority owner of Raritan Center Business Park, located in Middlesex County, N.J. With them, I developed an energy efficiency and renewables program to upgrade their existing real estate portfolio. My work with customers such as Sysco Foods, L'Oreal, Fuji Film, and Baccarat has given me firsthand experience with energy efficiency and controls, project management, HVAC and renewables, and practically every other property management tool. I also have a thorough understanding of some of the most sophisticated, energy-efficient, renewable and alternative-fuel technology and strategies utilized in real estate and fleet operations.

Among my accomplishments, I have successfully managed sales and marketing strategies ranging from start-up operations to the nation's premier business park, consisting of more than 15 MM square feet of commercial, industrial and flex space. I have created and managed successful projects for companies such as British Airways World Cargo, Cadbury Schweppes and Phoenix Beverage. I have also initiated improvements such as the utilization of local, state, utility and federal grant and incentive programs to maximize project size and scope, creation and implementation of a policy and procedure manual, and productive owner / tenant retention and incentive programs.

The reason I am here is that I want to make a career shift to full-time energy sales. I believe that my skills and experience would fit well into this field, and that I can also make an immediate contribution. I can be especially effective at insuring customer retention, cold-calling, and operating a cost-effective sales campaign, as well as enhance the value of marketing efforts.

I can also contribute the perspective that only experience can provide, as well as a professional, ethical and enthusiastic attitude.

Example: Direct-Mail Letter based on the above two-minute pitch

March 17, 2013

Mr. Michael Jan Smith, SVP & CFO
Glaxo-Wellcome Inc.
5 Moore Drive
Research Triangle Park, NC 27709

Dear Mr. Smith:

I am aware that your company is in need of successful FINANCIAL / OPERATIONS EXECUTIVES.

For more than 13 years, I have been solving major business process issues at the senior level. I have done this in the areas of sales, finance and operations. My main expertise is in strategic and tactical planning, productivity accomplishment, business process redesign, and financial management and reporting.

As a regional finance director for a major food corporation, one of the most successful consumer-packaged goods companies in the world, I developed a thorough understanding of managing the business process, including long-range strategic planning, short-term goal setting, and action planning, along with cost-control methodologies.

Among my accomplishments, I have:

- Created strategic visions and fact-based selling plans that successfully developed the business and increased market share in the New York region from $135 million to $266 million, and 28% to 49% in only five years.

- Strengthened supply-chain efficiency by facilitating a series of planning meetings between Sales, Operations and Finance. Created a jointly owned performance scorecard and rearranged job accountabilities.

- Prepared business analysis with specific recommendations that improved profit margin by 0.7% or $2.9 million annually.

- Implemented local coaching initiatives using tracking, analysis and reporting tools that beat aggressive cost targets by more than $635,000.

I am now looking for an opportunity where I can leverage my skills and experience in a larger role. I can be particularly effective at developing and achieving a company's business plan. I also bring a professional, ethical, and enthusiastic attitude in everything I do.

My resume is enclosed. I would be glad to discuss my experience further in a personal interview.

Very truly yours,

Anthony T. Walsh
609-555-5555

4. Networking Backward

Most people know the story about the out-of-town couple that came to New York City for the first time and asked their cab driver how to get to Carnegie Hall. The cab driver replied: "Practice, lady, practice." That is exactly how you get good at networking—through practice. When working your business and professional contacts, however, you need to network backward; i.e., with your least important contacts first. I call them your "C" grade contacts, then move up to the "B" grade contacts, and finally meeting with your best or "A" grade contacts. In other words: Don't practice with your "good stuff."

It is a grave mistake to leave a job and start calling your best contacts, those that work for world-class employers, such as Goldman Sachs, Apple, or Johnson & Johnson. You're not ready to meet with these contacts, because you have not defined the product that you're selling (your skill set and experience), your resume is not updated and polished, and you have not defined where you want to go next.

Placing yourself in front of your best contacts without adequate preparation is a sure way to unnecessarily extend your job search. Don't do it. Instead work your contacts from "C" to "B," then to your "A" contacts.

Finally, it is good to remember the terrific quote from Vince Lombardi: "Luck is preparation meeting opportunity." Thomas Jefferson said it a little differently: "I am a great believer in luck, and the harder I work, the more I have of it." Instead of being in a hurry and simply making yourself feel better with a flurry of uncoordinated activity, with proper preparation, you will be able to maximize the number of interviews, and then interview at a more opportune time. In addition, you will also make it easier for your networking contacts to help you, because you are better prepared.

5. Networking Support Material

When people network one-on-one with a colleague or a personal recommendation, they usually discuss their situation: where they were, why they are in job transition, and what they're looking for next. Though they will give their contact a copy of their current resume, the job hunter is hoping their contact takes notes or remembers what was discussed. In most cases, your contact won't take notes, and will forget what you discussed after a single day. So what good was the meeting? Maybe you received a lead or two.

The key sales concept of "make it easy for your customer to buy" provides you with a better way: Put your basic job-search needs *in writing*. Below is an example of a written networking summary for use during the networking meeting, and to accompany a copy of your resume. It can also be used via the Internet and telephone. It provides all the pertinent information your contact will need, in the weeks and months ahead, to evaluate any leads appropriate for you.

Below is an example of the written **Networking Handout** that you would use during one-on-one meetings.

Elements of a **Networking Handout**:

Part 1. Status Update. Where you stand in your job search.
Part 2. Reminder they may come across valuable information.
Part 3. Professional Summary
    A. One paragraph. Identify what you are (your handle), and what expertise you will bring to a new employer. How you add **value**.
Part 4. Positioning/How You Are Targeting Industries and Companies; geographic limitations.

Part 5. Positions Wanted. Use categories of positions, i.e., type of consulting, level of position.

Part 6. Characteristics of Good Leads. Be very specific and eliminate all ambiguity. Areas to cover include people, companies, divisions of companies, foreign or domestic, business and trade articles on the area you are targeting, individual names of people in companies, executive search firms, employment agencies, and publications.

Part 7. Close. How you will reciprocate.

Sample Networking Handout

Test Sample Name

1 Example Avenue
Tester, State xxxxx
1.xxx.xxx.xxxx TSample@mail.com

Ms./Mr. Name, Title   Date
Company
Street
City, State ZIP

Update: I have been separated from Lowenstein Sandler PC, and would appreciate your help. I have made substantial progress on my employment search, and am talking with several companies about positions. Even so, I am still seeking a totally suitable match, and would appreciate any leads you may have.

You may have a contact or two who would help me network to the right person. I would appreciate names of individuals, or introductions to acquaintances with possible contacts.

My Value: I am a LITIGATION PARALEGAL/ IT ANALYST with a proven history of success. For more than 13 years, I have been solving legal and accounting business issues at the paralegal/analyst level. I have done this in the areas of litigation and accounting systems. My main expertise is in litigation, project management, technical support, IT end-user support, and quality assurance and process improvement.

Target Industries: Ideally, I am looking for a position with an organization in New Jersey, a law office, or corporation in New Jersey, with a requirement of one to three years' legal and/or more than five years' corporate experience. Typical companies might include:

- **Law Offices:** Small to midsize Business Law firms
- **Accounting Firms:** Ernst & Young, Deloitte Consulting, PriceWaterhouseCoopers, KPMG
- **Telecommunications Companies:**Verizon Wireless, Vonage, Virgin Mobile
- **Medical/Pharmaceutical**: J&J, Merck, Novartis

Relevant leads would include:

- Contacts/ acquaintances within the companies listed above
- Contacts in other like companies
- Business-news articles related to my target industries.

Your offer to assist me is sincerely appreciated. Since networking is a two-way street. I also have an extensive business network, and I am prepared to return the courtesy whenever needed.

Sincerely,

P.S.: Please use the blank form and return it to me in the pre-addressed stamped envelope.

Contact Information Instructions:

1. Set aside a few minutes to look up people you know who fit the job industry profile I'm seeking.

2. Check your personal phone book, any business cards you may have, and your email.

3. Note the name of the person, title, company, and contact information.

4. Please return this to me in the pre-addressed stamped envelope or via email.

I will follow up with you to get more information before I introduce myself to any of your contacts.

Thanks a million.

Name	Title	Company	Phone
Name	Title	Company	Phone
Name	Title	Company	Phone
Name	Title	Company	Phone

* * *

6. **Thank-You Letter model**—see pp. 205-207.

7. **Developing mailing lists**

Your best source is the Internet (Google) and the research department in the local county library, university library or big-city library. Additional sources include *Crain's New York Business Book of Lists* and *NJBIZ Book of Lists* in the New York City metro area. Also check out the Corporate Finance Sourcebook and the Corporate Finance Bluebook. Many local business publications publish a "Book of Lists." Check them out.

8. The best source for recruiter mailing lists is the Recruiting & Search Report out of Panama City, Florida. Below is contact information. This data supplier is highly recommended because it updates its data files monthly.

The Recruiting & Search Report
P.O. Box 9433
Panama City, Florida 32417
www.rsronline.com

Now that you have your job-search support materials prepared, along with your newly created marketing resume, let's look at the mechanics of job search. You can look for a new position in just four ways – ads and the Internet, employment agencies and executive-search firms, the "hidden job market," and networking. Let's review each in some detail.

Ads and the Internet

The supply of newspaper-based want ads has largely disappeared with the advent of the Internet. Yet each year, on the effectiveness of Internet ads, research consistently shows that they fill only 3 percent of available openings. The Internet has proved helpful for low-level IT and administrative types, but not for middle managers or senior-level executives. Putting a majority of your time and effort into Internet search sites and company job boards will not be very productive, and forces you to compete against thousands of candidates.

One print advertising area that can be fruitful is industry-specific publications like *Chemical Week* and *Advertising Age*. Companies recruiting for experienced talent in these industries will usually advertise in industry-specific publications.

You Don't Have to Be Fully Qualified to Respond to a Want Ad!

Many people, during their careers, and particularly during the job-search process, are under the mistaken impression that to qualify for the listed specifications in a want ad, you need to meet all of the requirements—especially if the qualifications are identified as "required" in the advertisement. In reality, this is *not* true.

It is important to understand how a job advertisement is created. For most organizations, the process is generally simple, and doesn't require a lot of effort. A recruiter from human resources will sit down with the hiring manager and question the person regarding his or her requirements for the job. In most cases, the requirements come from the executive's experience with the job responsibilities, and fall into two categories: those the executive "must have" and those they "prefer to have." Example:

MUST PREFERRED

MUST	PREFERRED
3-5 years of experience	4-7 years of experience
Bachelor's degree	Masters (MBA)
Health and Beauty Aid experience	Vitamin experience
Etc.	Etc.

The HR recruiter then conveniently drops both columns of requirements into the **want ad**. This is what they want! But since few candidates exist that have *all* the "'necessary" requirements, the company executive and the human resources department have to compromise on their expectations.

In reality, most companies will compromise on their requirements and accept less than the ad states. This is because very few candidates have all of the listed requirements, and to wait and leave the position open too long antagonizes the hiring executive and costs the company too much in money, productivity and morale.

Some years ago, I counseled a customer service manager from the technology group of a large bank supporting the brokerage industry. Some weeks after completing this client's marketing resume and counseling, I noticed an ad in *The Wall Street Journal* for a product manager at a small software-development firm serving large financial institutions. The requirements in the ad closely matched my client's background and experience, so I answered the ad using a "blind" version of his marketing resume—one that did not identify the person or his employer by name. He got the interview and subsequently was hired into the position, despite the fact that the ad said "MBA preferred." My client had only 50 credits. An associate's degree requires 60 credits.

The explanation for why my candidate was hired turned out to be simple. The company knew what it wanted (it was contained in the want ad), but not what it needed. My candidate's resume represented what the company needed—experience, skills and the ability to **fit**. It then forgot what it wanted—an MBA.

Employment Agencies and Retained-Search Firms

Each type of external recruiting firm functions differently.

Contingency firms, better known as **employment agencies**, recruit for positions up to $100,000 and only receive payment contingent upon hiring of their candidate. All their efforts and expenses come out of their own pocket, based on speculation that their candidate will be hired.

Retained Search firms, better known as headhunters or **executive search** firms, function like attorneys. They do nothing on speculation, but instead sign an agreement with the company that wants to fill a position. They receive a third of the successful candidate's base salary, plus expenses, whether or not the company hires any of the candidates they present. Retained-search firms generally fill positions over $100,000 only, and will not represent candidates earning much less than $100,000. On occasion, if you have a solid background and an impressive resume (the marketing resume), retained search recruiters will sometimes offer these candidates as a "freebie" to good clients and not charge anything.

For both the contingent and retained-search recruiters, the placement fee is always company-paid. Walk away from any recruiter that demands you pay anything.

Attacking the "Hidden" Job Market: Using Direct Mailings

More than two-thirds or 67 percent of all job openings are either never advertised or placed with a recruiting firm. So how are these jobs filled? Usually through the "Old Boy" or "Old Girl" network (i.e., who do you know?). Also, because networking is somewhat inefficient and extremely time-consuming, the better and more efficient way to tap the hidden job market is through a direct-mail strategy.

* * *

Reprinted from the *Wall Street Journal's National Business Employment Weekly*

Job Search Strategies

How Direct Mail Can Excite Hiring Managers
Marketing letters are usually more effective than resumes

by Lloyd Feinstein

Editor's Note: In his article last week, Mr. Feinstein discussed the importance of viewing a job search like a sales problem, with the hiring manager as customer and you as the product and salesperson. He also described the Problem-Action-Result (PAR) method of illustrating accomplishments and experience in written marketing materials. This week, Mr. Feinstein explains how to prepare direct-mail letters that impress hiring managers.

Part II of II

The secret to landing new positions is showing future employers that it pays to hire you. Therefore, your marketing materials must "ring the cash register" by clearly demonstrating how an employer will benefit from offering you a job.

To be successful at this strategy, though, you must understand and emphasize the hiring managers' needs, not your own. In other words, view your search like a sales campaign and think like your customers.

Since resumes often are ignored or returned to Human Resources, it's wise to use effective marketing devices when communicating with hiring managers. The following is a guide to preparing marketing materials that interviewers are likely to read.

Getting Past Gatekeepers

When responding to classified ads, most job hunters are asked to send a resume, cover letter and salary history. *Never* send your salary history, since it's merely a Human Resources screening device. If your history doesn't match the range for the available position, you'll be eliminated.

But even if you send a resume and cover letter directly to a hiring manager, how do you know your materials will be read? Don't most secretaries and administrative assistants automatically send resumes to Human Resources departments?

The solution to getting past them is to send a marketing letter using direct-mail principles. The following direct-mail formula developed by Richard C. Bordon, a New York University professor, is the basis for all U.S. advertising, including most of the junk mail you receive. It includes four elements:

1. The hook. A paragraph that describes the employer's greatest need.

2. Why you're mentioning it. This section typically starts with a sentence beginning with, "I am writing because…"

3. For instance. Additional paragraphs that describe your effectiveness and accomplishments. They should be bulleted or indented for emphasis and match the employer's <u>critical</u> needs.

4. So what? What you want the reader to do, such as offer an interview.

To prepare your marketing letters, review the accompanying sample. Since it's only one page, it's more likely to survive the administrative assistant and be read by a busy hiring manager.

A Letter's Benefits

Note that the letter quickly answers the manager's first question, "What's in it for me?" by showing that you can solve a pressing problem. Then, in the following paragraphs, you explain how several generic problems were resolved. At the very least, managers view interviews as a way to gain free consulting advice. After receiving your letter, those who don't call to schedule a meeting are ignoring their own self-interest.

The letter also deliberately indicates a candidate's approximate age by including educational degree dates. However, regardless of the age issue, hiring managers are likely to favor him or her because the letter answers critical hiring questions: Can the candidate do the job, solve pressing problems and help the employer save or make money?

Remember, the key is matching a target employer's greatest needs with your best accomplishments. Always emphasize and expand on the positive aspects of your work history, while reducing or eliminating any negatives that might work against you in the hiring process. Your ultimate goal is to gain an interview invitation. Then, if the interviewer determines that your personality fits the organization, you may be offered a position.

Always emphasize the positive aspects of your work history while eliminating any negatives.

Finally, since different managers have unique needs, create several versions of your letter by reconstructing and adjusting the paragraphs.

The beauty of a well-written marketing letter is that it serves as a functional resume without actually being one. It shows off your most impressive career achievements, but not necessarily in order or at only one employer. For instance, each of the problems a candidate solved could have occurred at different companies.

There's no doubt that marketing letters are effective. I used one to change from a training and personnel position with a nonprofit hospital to a training management job with Cadence Industries Corp., a for-profit $120 million diversified company in West Caldwell, N.J.

When the position was advertised. I sent a letter to the manager specified in the ad. I later interviewed with David Balaban, then director of Human Resources at Cadence, and now senior vice president with Daniel Silverstein Associates, an executive search firm in East Brunswick, N.J. Mr. Balaban said recently that he thought I had sent him a resume. Instead, the letter alone was the basis for my interviews with Cadence managers and my subsequent hire.

Although I didn't need a resume to land my Cadence job, most hiring managers aren't comfortable scheduling an interview until they receive one. Use similar problem-action-results statements on your resume, but don't send it to the hiring manager. Too often, extraneous resume information that doesn't relate to the employer's immediate needs can be used to screen you out.

Instead, bring your resume to the meeting and emphasize how your accomplishments fit the employer's objectives. Also, try to demonstrate that your personality and style fit that of the current management team.

Unfortunately, in any job market, the most successful candidates are those who are perceived as the most qualified, even if that isn't the case. You may be the best candidate, so use a customer-oriented approach to your job search, to ensure that you're viewed that way.

Sample Direct Mailing Letter
For a Heating/Ventilation/Air Conditioning Chief Engineer

Hiring Manager
Title
Company
Street
City, State, ZIP code

Dear ---------------:

To reduce fumes in a 750,000 sq. ft. municipal garage, I added direct gas-fired burners to the rooftop package, instead of putting a large number of indirect gas-fired furnaces on the large energy-recovery system. Result: eliminated the need to add 200 inches to each of 12 rooftop packages; saved $20,400 per unit (total savings of $244,800); and reduced the overall length of each package to 20' from 36'.

I am writing because your organization may need a profit-oriented engineering professional with my background and experience. I am currently vice president of engineering for a $13 million division of a large, privately held industrial corporation. You may find the following accomplishments of interest.

- To stay competitive while maintaining the integrity of our product lines and profit margins, I demonstrated the salient features of our equipment, and how they compared with competing products, to consulting engineers and customers. Designed special features into our products to "lock out" our competitors. **Result:** convinced customers that our products, and field service repairs if necessary, were superior; over a five-year period, 52% of all bids were successfully converted into sales orders. This represented 24% of the company's business during this period.

- To reduce costs associated with the fabrication of our product lines, I assessed our products using value-analysis techniques. Made extensive structural design changes, reduced assembly-time labor costs and employed commonality of parts. **Result:** after two years, contributed over $216,000 toward the profit base of $315,000 that year. Direct contributions to profits have continued to be realized over the last two years.

- To satisfy top management's, internal sales' and the manufacturing department's requests for design drawings on a more timely basis, I interviewed managers and supervisors, then created and implemented a priority system to log and track requests. Established priorities based on customer delivery requirements, and color-coded orders for quick identification. **Result:** turnaround time reduced to two weeks from four weeks, and eliminated the one- to-four-week delay caused by the credit department.

- Interviewed, hired and trained a graduating engineer. After a three-year period, he was promoted to chief engineer in charge of bills of material and applications.

I have received my MME from Stevens Institute in 1974 and a ME in 1963. My salary requirements are competitive. I will call you in a few days to make an appointment for us to discuss my experience further in a personal interview.

Very truly yours,

* * *

Evidence of Direct-Mail Effectiveness

Story

Some years ago, working with a marketing communications executive, I discovered that the client wanted to work for Apple Computer. So I suggested he write a direct-mail letter to Steve Jobs, who was then head of the company. The client, however, doubted that Mr. Jobs would ever get his letter. So, I had to first convince this client of the validity of the direct-mail strategy. Here's what I told him.

When an executive is promoted up the corporate ladder, he or she must learn one business skill in spades, and that skill is the ability to *delegate* the work properly. What is interesting is that the executive will always delegate *everything*, with two exceptions:

1. the ability to hire and fire, because that's where the power lies, and
2. the ability to go through their mail uncensored, because whoever controls the information flow will control the executive.

So I argued that if he sends a one-page direct marketing letter with no resume, the letter would get into the executive's daily pile of mail. In that situation, your letter would get 10 seconds of the executive's time. Therefore, the first paragraph of any direct-mail piece is the most important component. His problem was to craft an opening paragraph that would resonate with Mr. Jobs. My client chose to argue that at the time Apple didn't know how to market their computers to home-based businesses.

Three weeks after mailing the letter, my client received a call from Apple's senior vice president of worldwide corporate communications. The first words out of her mouth were: "Your letter to Mr. Jobs was forwarded to my attention." After a brief conversation, the Apple executive set up an interview appointment at the MacWorld convention at the Javits Center in New York City. The interview was successful, and my client received a job offer, which he happily accepted.

Bottom line: Direct mail works because you have no competition, and it is a non-resume strategy that bypasses the HR department's screening process.

* * *

WHERE THE JOBS ARE AND HOW TO LAND THEM!

Plan For a Long Job Search.

Some bad information.

Even during the holiday season, the business press publishes bad information that undermines job seeker's fragile confidence and hampers their search activities.

In the *New York Times* business section , a book reviewer quoted from a recently published "work of literature": "People over 50 are walking liabilities." What unadulterated horse cr*p!

This kind of negative thinking is typical of the narrow, conventional and candidate-centered approach we hear at networking groups, in outplacement programs, and from the business press.

Continuing your job-search campaign with a "What's In It for Me" orientation (i.e. candidate-centric) rather than a "What the hiring person wants to buy" (client-centric) approach will only prolong your job search unnecessarily. There is a better way, a way that works, even in a difficult economy.

THE VIEW FROM THE HIRING DESK—Fourth-Quarter Perspective.

Holiday Myths

1. By the end of September each year, companies have three-quarters of their earnings in place, and are in the best position to do their manpower and succession planning. Budget dollars not used are often returned, and next year's departmental budget will likely be reduced by that amount. So, there is a selfish reason for managers to use their budget allocations, conditions permitting.

2. In those companies with a hiring freeze, other reasons continue to drive the interviewing and hiring process. Executives understand that their key employees will not leave the company until *after* they collect their bonuses—usually from the end of December through the middle of February. This being the case, management needs to have talented prospects in the

interview and hiring pipeline, if only as a potential backup in case of the loss of any critical employees.

Executive managers and recruiting executives always retain the resumes of candidates that look exceptional on paper. Plan your job search based on this factor.

Remember when you ran a department? You didn't throw away resumes of exceptional candidates. They were stored for future reference. You need to plan your job-search strategies to take advantage of this pattern of resume retention, because everyone does it. The question for people in transition should be: What is next to do? Let me give you an added sense of perspective and an additional job-search strategy *that works*.

The strategy that best maximizes the above conditions is writing directly to prospective employers. To make sure that you're in the executive's reference resume folder, you must think on how decisions are actually made. When an executive needs to interview to fill a key position, he goes with the candidates who come to mind when the need arises: those in the reference resume folder. Therefore, by "staying in front" of prospective executives on a regular basis, you can position yourself for when the right moment inevitably arises.

Next Issue

How to get into the reference resume folder? Answer: OPJs. Most executives are familiar with OPMs or Other People's Money. OPJs represent Other People's Jobs. It is not necessary to wait for an OPJ to open. Simply assume that the position you desire will become available due to promotion, resignation, firing, consolidation, merger, or poor performance. According to the business press, including *CFO Magazine*, the average senior financial executive's position turns over every 18 months. Assuming the job you want is in play is a fair bet.

This strategy opens up a whole new vantage point for viewing the job search: one that is **proactive** rather than reactive. And there is no need to feel any sense of guilt because you're targeting someone else's job. From both a business and career perspective, you're really doing all three parties a favor. You get the next right position (hopefully) for your career. The employer replaces a marginal performer and receives greater benefits. And the displaced employee has an opportunity to correct his/her deficiencies at his or her next employer.

Having been a director of human resources for some substantial companies, one of the strongest patterns I saw was that two-thirds of all positions my department recruited for were newly created positions. This pattern held regardless of economic conditions. The need to fill a position always starts first in the minds of hiring executives. Therefore, you need to act on this pattern. And the only efficient way to interact at the beginning of the hiring process is via mailings directly to the hiring executives.

What You Should Do

In an editorial that ran in January 2001, Matt Bud of the Financial Executive Network Group wrote that "Like any other major task, finding another work opportunity needs to be broken down into bite-sized pieces for easy digestion." And "step one is …the creation of a killer resume, killer cover letters, a killer 90-second announcement, development of a target company list, making a list of business associates to contact for networking, etc." Basically, you need to put together a set of marketing materials, especially the marketing resume and standalone marketing letters that use the Problem-Action-Result methodology. Because this approach is strongly customer-oriented, you're starting out by discussing the reader's problem, and will achieve a greater response rate than traditional job-search materials.

Once you have completed the self-assessment process and converted your accomplishments into PAR paragraphs, employ a two-step strategy in your search.

Step One: Use a direct marketing letter, *one page maximum*, written in the Problem-Action-Result format to generate telephone calls from employers interested in your background and experience. See the article entitled "Five Strategies for Outsmarting the Telephone Interview" at the end of this chapter.

Step Two: Use a Problem-Action-Result based resume to obtain the interview and distinguish yourself from the competition.

I know this two-step strategy works because I used it during my own career. In addition, my clients have success with this approach even in a recessionary job market. A client recently was coming off a seven-year period of entrepreneurship/consulting and desired to work full-time for an apparel company because she needed the structure. We created a single, one-page marketing letter that contained six paragraphs, four in the Problem-Action-Result format. The results were terrific: She mailed out 12 letters and received five interviews within a four-week period. In addition, regarding the company that hired her, she emailed me that "I never even gave them my resume!!!!!"

The direct-mail process works because of a number of important factors.

1. Since you're sending a letter, it will usually get past gatekeepers and will be read by the hiring executive; at least the first 10 seconds of your letter will be.
2. The direct-mail approach bypasses the human resources department. The hiring executive doesn't have to fill out a job requisition or work with HR during most of the hiring process. A plus for both you and the hiring executive.
3. There is no recruitment fee, which can be a stumbling block.
4. Your letter is focused on the business needs of the hiring executive; assuming your PARs reflect the universal needs of the industry you're targeting.
5. And finally, if your marketing letter is PAR based, it focuses on the only real issue in any job market: the hiring executive's needs or problems.

Where Can a Person's Skills / Experience Be Employed?

Some years ago I conceived a simple and inexpensive solution to this dilemma. This technique for evaluating possible employment opportunities was developed and appeared in a book I co-authored with Linda Kline, *Career Changing: The Worry-Free Guide*, published by Little, Brown & Co. in 1982. Called the want-ad analysis technique, it is used to define pertinent job content and other critical parameters for any job title.

The technique is simply a frequency analysis. Here's how it works. Collect a sample of 10 ads, all in the same job description, not job title. Then do a frequency analysis of the elements in all the ads. Using the form below, the technique will quickly help you determine if you're qualified:

- to apply for any position
- what jargon you should use in your marketing resume
- which job accomplishments to emphasize
- what industries the job is in
- what job titles you might qualify for.

Try the technique. It will allow you to do career exploration right from the Internet.

In summary

- avoid negative thinking
- be proactive
- go after OPJs using direct-mail techniques
- use PAR-based marketing letters to generate interviews, and PAR-based marketing resumes to close the deal
- remember that you're "selling the future": your confidence in being able to get the job done.

Final note:

Two important trends experienced by my clients over the last few years indicated the following:

First, most clients felt strongly the importance of having powerful "sales" (interview) support materials when trying to close the sale. The materials we prepared and used included long thank-you letters (between two and six pages), Best Candidate for the Job summary, "Get the Job By Doing the Job" two-page proposal, and assistance with salary negotiation.

Second, **all** of my clients who connected into a new position obtained a compensation package that was equal to or greater than their previous package. Companies are not trying to hire talent on the cheap. They will pay top dollar for talent that is perceived as first-rate. The key word here is *perceived.*

* * *

Overqualified—A common problem in job search

In counseling an executive recently, the common problem of being overqualified surfaced. He had interviewed in person with two different executive search consultants (headhunters), and was told that his background and experience, not to mention his compensation, were stronger than the specifications for the position. As a result, he was not considered further.

He was not sure how to respond to this situation. Though this is a difficult situation and is frequently used by recruiters for disqualifying candidates, strategies exist to deal with it. As background for this discussion, remember it is very dangerous to be willing to reduce your compensation level to meet the salary requirements for any position. You are undercutting your value to a future employer.

Our resume presentation was the main reason you were brought in for the interview. To accept a lower salary undercuts your value.

Imagine taking a friend to the local fur vault in an upscale shopping mall and seeing a full-length mink coat at a one-day special price of only $1,100. Your friend might get all excited, but your response would probably be: If this coat is so good, why is it so cheap?

The same question occurs during the interview process. If you are both excellent on paper and during the interview, why are you willing to take less? Only one reasonable answer: because you aren't as good as you say. This is a dangerous strategy, because it will undermine your position during the salary-negotiation process and also puts your accomplishments into question.

A better approach is to try and communicate how your **value** extends beyond the job specifications. Though the position specifications may concentrate on traditional responsibilities, it is to your advantage to review how your experience and expertise also include operations, M&A, compliance, new-business development, etc. Think "outside the box" and, also talk outside the box. Demonstrate in the interview that your expertise extends outside the position's usual responsibilities .

Perhaps your most important strategy in the interview is to **listen** carefully to what the interviewer is saying, and to identify their specific business needs. Their needs could be a specific problem that the organization is wrestling with, or an opportunity that they can take advantage of, if they possessed your skill set. Once you've listened and identified their problems or needs, then match it with a pertinent accomplishment that you achieved, and discuss your solution using the PAR method.

This whole process is very conversational. It should flow naturally, as with any conversation. In this way, you come across as an attentive listener whose experience directly matches their business needs To repeat, your strategy during the interview is to **listen** to their need or problem, **match** your pertinent accomplishment to their problem, and then **discuss** your accomplishment using the PAR method.

When demonstrating how you bring value to a company, be sure to tell appropriate examples of your substantial accomplishments. Your main objective in the interview is to demonstrate that you are the best *business* person for the position, not the best *technical* candidate.

These PA-R examples show the power of this method.

Basic:

Before: From a Business Manager, Chemical Industry

- Small Customer program increased sales $3MM/year with 50% gross margin. Implemented strategy and sales program.

After applying marketing resume (PAR) concepts:

- To improve margins, performed detailed profit and margin analyses on customer base. Convinced both sales and distribution organization to shift selling mix to smaller volume businesses. **Result**: small volume sales increased from $1 million to $6 million in three years at 50% gross margin.

Advanced:

Before: From a major national outplacement firm

- Implemented organizational and personnel changes resulting in improved morale and increased productivity. Dramatically reduced high employee turnover level.

After applying marketing resume concepts:

- To turn around the accounting department (120 employees), interviewed entire staff and established high visibility. Identified issues and bottlenecks. Developed and implemented a comprehensive reorganization, including job restructuring, personnel training and development, and wage and salary review. **Result**: eliminated professional OT and increased salaries, which saved $32K; turnover dropped from 34% to 12% in 18 months; productivity and morale increased dramatically; absorbed 10% increase in business activity without increasing staff.

Advanced:

Before: From a Business Systems Analyst for a large financial services corporation.

- Performed ongoing quality assurance testing and user training for listed and OTC equity trading systems.

After applying marketing resume concepts:

- To expand the equity listed and OTC desk use of business development services, worked with traders to outline and prioritize current problems and/or desired enhancements to the two systems. Tested and implemented all system fixes and enhancements. Provided comprehensive (16-48 hour) training for users. **Result**: built strong relationship with trading desk to ensure the business systems group is maximizing its potential in the software development process; achieved 100% utilization of IT business development services.

This approach to dealing with the issue of being overqualified requires the interviewee to know the product they're selling, and to be able to discuss accomplishments using a method that sells easily with the listener, i.e., PAR. Unless you have a quiver of arrows representing your key business accomplishments, each in the PAR format, you won't be able to convince others of your added value. Instead, what many people end up doing is **winging it**. This unfocused approach often explains why you're able to get the interview, but unable to close the sale.

Using the value-added approach to get around the issue of being overqualified does not always work, especially with recruiters. Nevertheless, based upon my years of counseling experience, underselling yourself **never** works to your long-term career benefit. If you do accept lower pay than you were earning, you won't be able to catch up financially, based upon yearly percentage increases.

* * *

JOB SEARCH STRATEGIES

AUDIENCE	STRATEGY	MATERIALS	ACTION
1. Human resource department	Comply with HR Requirements	PAR-based cover letter;	Adjust marketing resume to satisfy HR requirements
a. Job boards		Marketing resume	
b. Admin. assts.			
c. Exec. sec'y.			

A human resource department has a mandate to control an organization's hiring process to prevent chaos, enforce federal and state employment regulations, and avoid lawsuits.
In this capacity, HR usually eliminates applicants and candidates.

Since only 3 percent of jobs are filled through the Internet, this method of job search is highly inefficient, and produces the greatest amount of competition.

The **job fair** is a better way to make an introduction to a company's HR department. Try and put more of your effort in this area.

* * *

2. Agencies			
Employment Agencies (contingent firms)	Proactive Mailings	PAR-based cover letter;	Mail unsolicited to 10 firms daily, five days weekly
		Marketing resume	Use MSWord mail-merge to achieve efficiencies
Executive Search (retained search firms) (headhunters)	Proactive Mailings	PAR-based cover letter;	

| | | Marketing resume | Mail unsolicited to 10 firms daily five days weekly (agency source above) |

Other than a career counselor, the external recruiter, either contingent or retained, is the only other person in a job search who can make a buck off of your efforts to find a new position.

Therefore, it is in your best interest to make the recruiter's job as easy as possible. This is exactly the objective of the **marketing resume**. Your resume should quickly answer the three concerns of most hiring executives; i.e., do the job, solve our problems, and fit.

In providing this information quickly and efficiently in your resume to recruiters, you're actually doing their job for them. Most recruiters would be happy to represent you as a candidate and quickly collect their fee from the employer. So why are you making it difficult for them to represent you? Get rid of any prejudice you have based on previous experience, and concentrate on providing them with the best possible **marketing resume**. Besides, using a marketing resume is one of the most efficient ways to cross from one industry to another. **Remember: An interviewer won't present you if they can't "sell" you.**

* * *

3. Companies; Corporations	Proactive mailings	Non-resume strategy	Mail unsolicited to five companies; after exhausting agency list, increase to 15
	Call company telephone receptionist for name and address	PAR-based direct mail letter	

Writing direct to the hiring executive is one of the best ways to avoid the thousands of job candidates using the Internet who are competing for jobs that are of interest to you. My clients continuously have success with this strategy.

In New Jersey, where the pharmaceutical industry is concentrated, conventional wisdom says that you can only obtain an interview through a company's website. Not true.

Story

A few years ago, Johnson & Johnson was interested in replacing the executive that ran their internal outplacement function. I applied for this position with only a single-page, direct "snail mail" marketing letter to the senior vice president of human resources. I got the interview with the SVP despite the prevailing conventional wisdom.

Direct mail works, but depends on the quality of your direct letter, the strength of your opening sentence, and the number of letters mailed or emailed out.

* * *

4. Nonprofit	Same as above	Same as above	Mail unsolicited to five organizations; after exhausting agency list, increase to 10 daily

Using a direct-mail strategy to supplement mailing a cover letter and marketing resume is a very effective way to generate interviews in the nonprofit venue—but do both; don't just use the resume or non-resume strategy. Also, it is perfectly OK to write to more than one hiring executive in a particular organization or company.

5. Networking	Ask for help from acquaintances	Two-page networking handout	Try to attend two network events weekly in person, and one job fair weekly

Who you know is still the best strategy for landing a new position. But don't depend on people you know. Put forth the greatest effort with acquaintances and strangers.

Quoting Malcolm Gladwell in *The Tipping Point* (p. 54): "There is a very good example of the way Connectors function in the work of sociologist Mark Granovetter's ... classic study, *Getting a Job*. He found that 56% of those he talked to found their job through a personal connection. Another 18.8% used formal means—ads, headhunters—and roughly 20% applied directly. This much is not surprising ... But, curiously, Granovetter found that of those personal connections, the majority were "weak ties." "People weren't getting their jobs through their friends. They were getting them through their acquaintances."

My advice has always been to depend on strangers. Family and friends will always disappoint. Adjust these models according to your audience.

* * *

Five Strategies for Outsmarting the *Telephone Interview*:
Critical First Hurdle in Landing a Job

Quick Initial Evaluator

The only purpose of a telephone interview is to do a quick screening of possible candidates before bringing them in for a face-to-face interview. Since the cost of travel is considerable for an out-of-the-area candidate, it is probably a valid approach.

Remember, you get only one chance, and making a good impression over the phone is harder than in person, because both parties are missing all visual cues.

Your goal is to be invited in for an in-person interview. Therefore, try your best to keep the call as brief as possible. Yet keep in mind that another of your goals is to sound smart.

Many candidates are unknowingly eliminated early in the hiring process because of unintentional errors committed during a brief phone-screening interview.

Prepare in Advance

The success rate of advancing from phone to personal interview is approximately 30 percent to 40 percent. You can increase your odds by planning for the call. Think about what your goals would be if you were the interviewer, and then prepare yourself to meet these goals.

Research the company on the web beforehand and study the position specifications. The preparation you need to do about the company is the same as if you were going there.

Do not use a cellphone or an early-model cordless phone. Use a late-model cordless phone with a new battery, or a landline with a long cord. If you have a poor or noisy phone connection, ask the interview for her or his number and offer to call them back.

Minimize distractions. If you will be at home, find a quiet place, away from distractions. You must be totally focused on your interviewer.

It is important to be organized. Have your resume out on your desk at all times and review it before a call comes in.

Make a list of the areas you feel you would like to cover, and check them off as you are able to communicate them.

Reasons Candidates are Eliminated After Phone Screenings

The phone interview can be a giant killer. Candidates who are perfect fits for great jobs are being eliminated after phone calls of 20 or 30 minutes' duration. Some of the typical feedback heard from hiring executives are that candidates:

- lack enthusiasm
- are unable to articulate themselves well
- fail to ask relevant questions
- seem disinterested
- sound awkward or uncomfortable
- can be heard gum chewing, smoking or eating

Remember that you also need to connect with the client's administrative assistant.

Strategies for Improving Your Phone Interview

Sharpen verbal skills. Learn to describe your value and accomplishments briefly, but effectively and to the point. Be able to create "word pictures" for your interviewer, to support their lack of seeing you. The best way is to use the Problem-Action-Result communication methodology. Also, numbers create excellent visual images.

Be honest. Be upbeat.

Conduct the interview in a standing position. Sitting during a telephone interview is not a good idea because your conversation will tend to lack energy. Walk around when you are on the phone. Being able to gesture will make you come across as more forceful.

Just as when you are speaking to a large audience, you may have to force yourself to speak a little slower than normal, more clearly, and perhaps even a little louder.

Practice being brief. Practice your elevator speech. Practice stating a brief summary of how you impacted a business, and why it was better for you having worked in it.

Listen carefully to your interviewer's questions. *Answer the question asked.* Provide amplification *only* when asked.

If you answer a question and the line falls silent, give your interviewer the opportunity to process your last statement, and take some notes. Unless you have a question, let them ask the next one.

Be willing to email and share work samples, and then review them together during the call.

Show interest, but don't show desperation. Politely ask your interviewer what the next step might be and when you may next hear from him or her.

Remember, during each phone interview, you are a sales representative.

End Game—Follow-up and Practice

After a phone interview, send a thank-you that recaps your best selling points.

If the phone interview does not lead to a personal meeting, try to analyze the call, and look for ways to improve your presentation in the next one.

Anything you do a lot will enable you to improve at it, even pitching your services over the phone. Like so many things, it's one of the skills we have to build to be good at job search, so don't avoid or dread it. It is all part of the game.

Final point: The face-to-face interview won't happen if you don't treat a phone interview with the same gravity.

* * *

VALUE-ADDED NETWORKING: A Three-Part Discussion
by Lloyd Feinstein

Part One: The Typical Networking Model, and Why It Limits Your Effectiveness.

In this three-part discussion, I will first cover the traditional networking model. Why its effectiveness is limited. Why executives are reluctant to use it. In the second and third parts, I will introduce an approach that has been used successfully for decades by sales professionals that will maximize your business-building relationship capabilities and overcome your reluctance to use this most critical of job-search techniques.

First, let me review the traditional networking model that has been recommended by outplacement firms and appeared in national publications over the last 20-30 years. The outline below appeared in the December 1998 business section of a regional newspaper. It is very typical of the advice job seekers come across on the topic of networking.

1. You need to establish a network of contacts because 65 to 80 percent of all jobs are found through networking. (This is true.)

2. Be prepared. Keep your business cards and copies of your resume with you all the time. (True)

193

3. Talk with your personal contacts first. Practice selling yourself to those closest to you before selling yourself to strangers. (False)

4. Begin contacting those people to whom your personal contacts referred you. Start each conversation by stating how you received their name. Put the person at ease by saying you know they don't have a position, but that you need their help with information and possible job leads. Try to establish a relationship by showing an interest in what they have to say. (False)

5. Ask for information, not a job. Use the "information interview" time wisely. In advance of the meeting, research the industry and company. Discuss companies you are targeting, and ask if the person knows anyone else in the industry with whom you could speak. Get permission to use their name and always say thank you. (True). *Insider's Tip*: Many executives are tired of one-to-one networking, but will give a minute or two on the phone.

6. Use each meeting to get the most information possible. Give your contact a brief summary of your career objective, major strengths and accomplishments. Then ask specific questions that will provide you with helpful information. (False)

7. Look for opportunities to reciprocate. Offer something of value to those who are taking time to help you. As you ask questions and listen to answers, respond with helpful information of your own. (<u>True, True, True</u>!)

8. Keep your promises. If you promise to call back, do it. (True)

9. Stay in touch. Keep your contacts informed about your job-search progress. Send a thank-you letter *within 24 hours* after every informational interview. (True)

Regardless of the source, the above elements seem to be the basis for most discussions on the topic of networking.

The difficulty with this model is that it is time-worn, and most executives know that it represents basically a one-way street. They receive little or no benefit from the time they spend with you. The networker, you, comes out of the meeting with useful information, but the person you met receives little or no value. Interestingly enough, both you and the person with whom you are networking know this. Perhaps this is the reason most middle-level and senior executives and professionals find networking so distasteful—and why they are so reluctant to pick up the telephone. Because they feel that they are basically begging and asking for a handout, and this puts them in a position of weakness and lacking in control. Feeling this way causes most job hunters to de-emphasize networking, and instead put most of their job search efforts into answering advertisements, contacting recruiters, or writing directly to companies or organizations.

Since the job seeker feels he or she has so little to offer, why did the executive agree to see him or her in the first place? Usually you are able to secure a meeting with a key executive because that person cannot afford to antagonize the person who recommended you to them. That referral person could be a major client, customer, supplier, or key industry leader. So they agree to see you, even if reluctantly. When you appear in their office, however, that contact now has two very distinct problems. First, the probability they have a position for you is just about nil. And second, how quickly can they get you out of their office without antagonizing you and the referral person? The way they do it is simple: they express excitement and give you the names of *two other people to contact*. And of course, you can use their name. **A waste of time for all**.

Excited with these new contacts, you leave their office and the process then repeats itself. When you meet with one of these new contacts, they have the exact same two problems that the referral contact had: They don't have a job to fit your needs, and seek how to get you out of their office without antagonizing the referral source. Guess what they do? You're right! They give you a few more referrals and the process continues. If you have experienced this type of networking, you understand that your "leads" grow geometrically. And your networking experience turns into a continuous psychological downer.

To keep their sanity, most people cut back and eventually do little or no networking. It is the only way they can protect their fragile self-confidence. After leaving their former employer and getting their fair share of rejections in the job search, the last thing most people want is the in-person rejection of this type of networking. Thankfully, there is a better networking model to use that comes from our friends who make a living selling things. See parts two and three for a full discussion.

Part Two: VALUE-ADDED NETWORKING—A More Effective Approach!

Concept: Learning to network as sales executives do, in a consulting capacity.

To overcome your reluctance to network, it is necessary that you first understand how sales professionals do it. The concept they use is quite simple: *you go first*! What this means is that in a sales-call network meeting, the sales person has to go first. They have to offer value to the person to whom they are talking. In this context, value could mean many things, but it refers usually to information related to marketplace needs, professional trends, target-industry trends, and industry gossip.

There are two other names for this approach to networking: "gifting" or "acting like a consultant." The key question you must answer in the networking scenario is: Why should the person talk to you? And the answer should always be the same: It is in their *business self-interest* to talk with you. You possess information that they need and can put to profitable or personal use. It is in their self-interest to talk with you and pick your brain. The beauty of this networking strategy is that the networker no longer is coming into the meeting with his hat in his hand. You are no longer looking for a handout. Rather, they come to the meeting offering value (information) and just as importantly, *they must go first.*

Let me illustrate. For most people, just picking up the telephone and making the networking call is the most difficult action, because they lack confidence, they don't wish to be rejected, and they feel they have little to offer. These uncertainties can be replaced with confidence by simply offering value to the person you're calling. For example:

Job Hunter/Steve Applegate:

Mr. Johnson, my name is Steve Applegate, and I was referred to you by your packaging supplier, Walter Howard of Pharmaceutical Packaging Corporation. I have been actively researching your industry: its recent technological changes, industry trends, personnel issues, etc., and am currently involved in a job search for a senior purchasing position. In addition, I have interviewed with two key competitors of your company (name them). I would like to share with you what my research has discovered and how it can benefit your company. At the end of our discussion, I would like to review my job-search efforts and how you could be of assistance. I would need only 30 minutes of your time. May I suggest either Thursday or Friday afternoon next week?

Would Mr. Johnson agree to meet with Steve Applegate? The chances are high that he would because Steve went first. He started his call by making a connection to Mr. Johnson through a mutual contact. Then he offered value in the form of up-to-date business information on competitors in Mr. Johnson's industry. Like most executives, Mr. Johnson doesn't have the time to stay current with what is happening daily in his business. The opportunity to quickly catch up in a personal conversation, where he can ask questions and doesn't have to do research or a lot of reading, is very appealing to busy executives.

This strategy assumes a few key points. First, during your job search, you should schedule your *interview backward.* That is, interview first with the "C" companies: those you wouldn't necessarily work for but would interview with to get experience. Then you would move up to interviewing with "B" companies: those middle companies that you would consider working for if the circumstances were right. Finally, you would then be in a position to interview with the "A" companies: these are companies that are recognized as industry leaders and world-class organizations. One way to get this sequence of interview experience is to sort the ads you answer into A, B, and C categories, then answer them backward. Do this by waiting a week between mailings. In this way, your interviews with "A" companies will come last.

The second strategy you must use is to research the company and its industry in great detail. Always start by reviewing *Standard & Poor's Industry Surveys*: two volumes of up-to-date data for all major domestic industries. Updated quarterly, each analysis covers prospects for a particular industry, historical presentation of trends and problems; and sales, earnings and market data for leading companies. Also, use the Internet to review the company's website, and research the company, including its 10Q & 10K, if it is a public firm (SEC EDGAR; https://www.sec.gov/edgar/searchedgar/companysearch.html).

Once you are in the door for your meeting, the structure of this type of networking meeting is really quite different from the traditional approach. After the usual pleasantries, the person you are meeting with is anxious to have you discuss what you've discovered in interviews and research efforts. This will occupy most of the time you have together. Go into great detail. Ask questions. Demonstrate the scope of your research and knowledge of his or her industry and company. At the end of your discussion, you should have:

1. impressed him or her with your knowledge.
2. provided much useful information/insights, and got his/her brain working.

At this point, the person with whom you are networking will express his/her appreciation and make an offer to help you. Since "you went first," it was now his/her turn to reciprocate if he/she expects you to stay in touch and continue to "gift" him/her with useful business information.

Part Three: Value-Added Networking

When they ask you how they can help you in your job search, here's how you respond.

1. First, take out a prepared list of the 10 top companies that you are targeting; probably all "A" companies. This list should contain the name, title and direct-line telephone number of two executives in each company that you want to meet.

2. Next, give the list to your networking contact and ask that he/she review the list. Ask if he/she knows any of the names on the list. If so, then ask if he/she would be willing to pick up the telephone and call that person to arrange a meeting. Insurance pros use this lead-generation technique. In most cases, your contact would be glad to make the call, because he/she wants to reciprocate for all the good information you provided him/her.

3. When your contact is speaking to one of the names on your list, he/she will probably be giving you a reference. At the same time, however, psychologically, he/she may be saying to him/herself that if you are as good as I say, why am I recommending you to another company or competitor? He/she would then think about ways to use your expertise in his/her own company. This is exactly what the job seeker wants.

A final point about value-added networking is the role played by your resume. Unlike traditional networking, the resume plays no active role whatsoever. Instead, it becomes a leave-behind device to strengthen their impression of you. This is especially true if you're using the PAR-based marketing resume.

In summary, to succeed at building business relationships, you need to know:

1. Who are you? Your style. How do you make things happen? Your core competencies, skills, interests, values, experiences, and your unique differentiators.

2. How others see you. Gain perspective from others. Determine if you are sending the right message. Are your listeners receiving the message? Do you have strengths you aren't using? What's your reputation?

3. What's your market? Marketplace needs. Professional trends. Target-industry trends. Future competencies and skills. Why people should talk to you.

4. What are your options? Professions/occupations to explore. Industries and organizations where your profession is core. Important themes for the future—what you want to do next. Goals. Ask questions that show you know their process.

5. Who do you need to meet? Decision makers. Critical linkages—attorneys, accountants, etc. Professional colleagues. Thought leaders. Search-firm connections. Business and personal relationships.

6. What are you selling? What do you bring to your targets? Why should people talk to you? What's in it for them? Are your focused? Have you planned your presentation? What do you want them to do?

7. Implementing your plan. Set goals for your networking. Have a planned personal presentation. Know how to ask what you need from people. Get comfortable with the concept—it's a life skill. Follow up, follow up, follow up. Keep the networking working.

And most important, get yourself in front of people who understand what you're talking about.

Value-added networking is based upon interviewing backward, strong research, you acting in a consulting role during your networking meeting, and offering valuable information first, then asking your contact to make calls on your behalf.

A few final thoughts: 1) job hunting is a contact sport; 2) think of networking as contact development; and 3) the biggest error, when networking, is *lack of follow-through*.

CHAPTER 11

KEY INTERVIEW and SALARY ISSUES

Remember your wonderful PAR stories?

This comes under the heading "live and learn." Most people know that one of my major career hallmarks is the use of the communications strategy called "PAR." I have been using PAR, which stands for Problem-Action-Result, in my own career since 1972, and in my counseling business since 1984. In addition, in my 1982 book, *Career Changing: The Worry-Free Guide*, published by Little, Brown & Co., a complete chapter was devoted to PAR methodology.

In 1988, McGraw-Hill published a book called *SPIN Selling* by Neil Rackham. SPIN stands for Situation, Problem, Implication and Need-Payoff. My immediate reaction was that someone had written a book on selling using the PAR method. So I ignored the book. After all, I was becoming an expert on the application of PAR method and therefore had no need to read about it.

Surprise! I was wrong. The book is really about looking at the entire selling process differently. And this includes the employment interview that is simply a sales call. Below is a quote from the book that presents an interesting way to look at the interviewing process. In making a distinction between a small-ticket sale and a major-account sale, the author tells the following story (p. 85-86):

"A very experienced and successful sales manager in the process-control industry was once asked to explain at a company conference how he had succeeded in selling a multimillion-dollar system to a major oil company. He said, "The most important thing to remember about really big sales is that you only play a small part in the selling. The real selling goes on in the account when you're not there—when the people you sold to go back and try to convince the others. I'm certain that the reason I succeeded was because I spent a lot of time trying to make sure the people I talked to knew how to sell for me.

I was like the director of a play. My work was during rehearsals: I wasn't on stage during the performance. Too many people in selling want to be great actors. My advice is that if you want to make really big sales, you've got to realize that even if you're a great performer, you won't be on stage for more than a fraction of the selling time. Unless you rehearse the rest of the cast, the show will be a flop."

The author concludes: "Most people with experience in major-account selling would agree with this analysis. It's obvious that a lot of selling goes on when you're not around, so the better you prepare your initial sponsors, the easier it will be for them to convince others in the account."

For most people, the interview process is major-account selling, because you're asking an employer to pay hundreds of thousands of dollars in salary, perks and benefits each year when they hire you. And yet most people approach the interview like they're selling a small-ticket item.

* * *

SEARCH EFFORTS STARTING TO GENERATE INTERVIEWS

I assume you did an intensive job-search effort to generate interviews by sending out between 20 and 25 pieces a day, Monday through Friday, to ads, job-board leads, direct mailings to external recruiters (contingent / retained), companies/organizations, and networking contacts. Now you're probably starting to get calls and email requests for further information, including arranging for in-person interviews.

The initial step in the human resources hiring process is usually a telephone interview. To be better prepared for this ubiquitous type of interview, again review the article entitled "Five Strategies for Outsmarting the Telephone Interview" at the end of Chapter 10. Also, be sure you have a copy of your two-minute pitch taped to the wall by your home phone so you can come across in a professional manner. And you must stand up to read the wall.

When scheduling an in-person interview, try to come in at the end of the HR's scheduling sequence. Remember the "pizza box" concept? Using your marketing resume allows you to be perceived as the best candidate, and this will give you some leverage to persuade the HR representative to grant your scheduling request. Now let's review how to better manage the interview process.

All interviews have three parts:

1. what you need to do *before* the interview,
2. what you need to do *during* the interview, and

3. what must be done *after* the interview.

INTERVIEW PREPARATION ACTIVITIES *(Before)*

To complete the necessary activities *before* the physical interview, you must be able to answer two questions: What do you know about us, and Why do you want to work for us? To intelligently answer both questions, you need to do a thorough piece of research on **both** the industry and company where you're interviewing.

1. **Researching an industry**. The best single source is *Standard & Poor's Industry Surveys* that comprises three volumes of up-to-date data for all major domestic industries. Trends and prospects are then followed with a historical review of trends and issues, and 25 percent of the industries are updated quarterly. You can obtain this reference source at a good local or county library. Call ahead. Some libraries have the **surveys online.**

2. **Researching a company**. Use the Internet. Review each public company's website, its annual report and 10K (see Edgar website), and several search engines, e.g., Google. For privately held companies, the task is more difficult. Two suggestions:

a. Call the library in the town where the company is located, and ask for the name of the local newspaper. Call the paper's editor and ask to review his/her "vertical file" of articles on the company.

b. Visit the company and the local "watering hole" one or two days prior to your interview. **Do some field research:** Before an interview, visit at lunch and see what the people coming in and out are wearing. **When in doubt, overdress:** If you're at an interview, you can always take off your jacket or remove your tie.

3. Bring at least two extra copies of your resume.

4. Ask permission to take brief notes, two or three words (e.g., obsolete inventory, excessive interest expense, etc.). Use this information to write a *"sales"* thank-you letter that reconstructs the key issues raised during the entire interview. A **sample thank-you letter** can be found at the end of this chapter.

5. Ask for the interviewer's business card. If none is available, ask the secretary to write the critical business-card information on a piece of paper for you as you leave.

6. And finally, always ask the **same first question**. Whether you're interviewing with the HR department, a recruiting/executive search firm, or with the hiring executive, you always ask the same first question.

How much time do we have?

This will allow you to properly pace yourself and not waste the limited time you probably have.

Note: The last question at an interview may be the most important. How you answer "Do you have any questions for me?" is critical. The worst answer may be to say you have no additional questions. This indicates that you either have not done much research in preparation for the interview, or that you may not be very interested in the position. **Always come prepared with several meaningful questions for the interviewer in response to that final question.**

MANAGING THE INTERVIEW PROCESS *(During)*

You've done the necessary company research, you've developed your marketing resume and know the product that you're selling, calculated the best time to take the interview, and are dressed properly for the interview.

Now it's time to begin managing the interview itself. After the small talk at the beginning of the interview, always ask the same first question: **How much time do we have**? Once this is explained to you, begin to pace yourself by using the simple and easily memorized **interview model** below.

Remember, an interview is simply a *sales call* and has only two elements:

1. Tell your story
2. Close the sale!

To **Tell Your Story**, use this simple diagram:

A. **Listen**---------------- Problems }-------------- **Match** your accomplishments with employer's needs and **discuss** using PAR

Needs
Situations
Opportunities

B. **Ask**
C. **Assume**-------------- generic/universal   based on research

Begin by listening for the interviewer's issues. If they share them with you, select a particular problem and match it to a similar accomplishment from your work history. Then discuss what you did to solve the issue using the PAR method. For example: Candidate—That's an interesting point, Ms. Lewis. I solved a very similar problem at my last employer. This was our situation:

Problem _____
Action I took to solve the issue _____
And the result was excellent; we were able to _____. By the way, this is an example of how I get the job done.

In the event the interviewer fails to share any issues or problems with you, they may instead ask the classic question:

Tell me about yourself?

Answer this question in one of three ways.

1. Talk off the top of your head about your background and experience. The problem with this response is that it usually fails to match the interviewer's/company's need.

2. Repeat your elevator or two-minute pitch. This response has the same weakness as #1.

3. Ask the interviewer where they are bleeding or hemorrhaging (pain points).

The most productive approach is to ask a question: Ms. Lewis, rather than me talk about aspects of my background that don't match your specific needs, if you would share with me those three to four issues that are keeping you up at night, I believe, based on my review of your job description, that I can give you a better night's sleep. (Always nice to inject a little humor.)

The approach of answering a question with a question will work some of the time, but not all the time. If the interviewer comes back and again asks you to "Tell me about yourself?" you then go to the third strategy of the interviewing model: you **assume** a universal or generic problem/issue based on your extensive research.

Say: "Based on my extensive research, your organization is probably struggling with ___(name issue)____. I've had experience solving that problem. Let me describe our situation at my previous employer that is very similar to that industry-wide issue (or some verbiage similar to this).

So to repeat, the interviewing model looks like this:

1. **Listen** for the interviewer's issues.
2. If he/she fails to share the company's issues, **ask** him/her where the organization is hurting.
3. If he/she again fails to share problems, then **assume** universal / generic issues based on your research.

Closing the Sale

Whether you want the job or not, your second objective during each interview is to close the sale. Remember, the only way to get good at interviewing is to interview as often as possible. Likewise, the only way to get good at salary negotiations is to **close on every interview**.

To close the sale, you must first be enthusiastic during the interview. You're selling the future, not the past. Remember, however, that your enthusiasm should be directed at your past accomplishments, not that you're interviewing with Google.

Next, review your research effort with the interviewer. Be prepared to "gift" them with industry gossip. If you're unable to uncover any useful gossip, share an article that is pertinent to the interviewer's position in their organization. One such article is Gary Hamel's "Strategy As Revolution," *Harvard Business Review*, reprint #96405.

At the end of the interview, be sure to do three things: Ask a few intelligent / pertinent questions, maneuver for another meeting, and always **ask for the job**.

1. Worth repeating: The last question at an interview may be the most important. How you answer "Do you have any questions for me?" is critical. The worst answer may be to say you have no additional questions. This indicates that you either have not done much research in preparation for the interview, or that you may not really be very interested in the position. Always come prepared with several meaningful questions for the interviewer in response to that final question.

2. Next, ask or maneuver for the next meeting or interview.

3. Finally, always **ask for the job! Whether you want the position or not, always ask for the job**, so you can practice your salary negotiations. Since it's always easier to negotiate for a position you don't want, practicing in these situations will prepare you for the tougher negotiations with the company you would love to join.

   a. The best way to ask for the job is to imagine that you're at the dinner table with your significant other, and you need to explain why you desire to accept a particular position. You should cover these issues:

   - Based on your experience and background, you can make a key contribution to the organization, especially in assisting and training other members in the department.

   - Being fully qualified and experienced, you can join the organization and hit the road running to provide immediate assistance.

   - Having interviewed with key members of the organization, you feel very comfortable and know there is a good "fit."

   - You feel you could come in and relieve key executives of some of their responsibilities very quickly.

   b. Therefore, I want very much to work with you and want you to make me a job offer.

After leaving the interview, find some place to sit down and expand the brief notes you took during your interview discussion. It's important to write a thank-you letter that recaps the key issues raised during the interview. If you're going to be passed along for another interview, excuse yourself (you had a lot of coffee) to use the facility. In the toilet, sit on the commode and expand your notes. After your second interview, find a place to sit and expand your second group of notes. Each interviewer **must** receive a custom thank-you that reconstructs your discussion. When you get home, while the conversations are still fresh, compose your thank-you letter or letters using the model presented at the end of this chapter.

SALARY NEGOTIATIONS *(After)*

Only two issues relate to salary: what you're earning, and what salary expectations you have. The definitive book on this topic for managers and executives is:

Perks and Parachutes: Negotiating Your Executive Employment Contract
by John Tarrant

John Tarrant is one of the few writers on human resource topics whose books are an interesting read. Whether you're an executive or not, you could benefit from his knowledge and advice.

The first issue related to salary is current compensation. The recruiter who contacts you will usually inquire about your compensation, and is listening for a number, a base salary. Instead, give her/him a paragraph, and in the paragraph, review your **total compensation package**. This package includes base salary, additional cash, and any perks and benefits, which are usually 20 to 30 percent of your base salary. Prepare the paragraph ahead of time, validate its accuracy, and then memorize your compensation package.

Concept: Try to condition the recruiter and/or interviewer that you think in terms of a *total compensation package*, not just base salary.

The second issue is your salary expectations. What compensation are you looking for in your next position? The best way to answer the expectation question is to give the organization a range, if that's possible. For example:

"I am currently interviewing for positions between

$_____(X)_____ and $_____(Y)_____."

Example: base = $50,000, total comp. = $75,000

X = total comp. times 1.2 = $90,000 ($75,000 X 1.2)

Y = X + $10,000 to $20,000 = $110,000 ($90,000 + $20,000)

Therefore: "I am currently interviewing for positions between $90,000 and $110,000."

Always try to phrase your salary responses in terms of total compensation, because it represents what you're really earning, and it's how serious professionals and executives think. But if the person insists on knowing your base salary, tell them.

Companies and organizations will always have strong arguments why they can't pay you what you want. They usually follow an established "salary range," and desire to hire at the bottom of the range. This way, it will take the longest period of time before a person needs to be promoted. Here are some of the reasons organizations give for not meeting your salary expectations.

- poor business climate / economy
- company had a tough year financially
- the amount you're asking for is above our salary range, and too close to what the supervisor of this position is making
- union contract restricts our salary flexibility

I'm sure you could add to this list.

Story

In the 1970s, I worked in New York City as director of training and assistant director of human resources for Bellevue Hospital Center, a 1.6 million-square-foot facility with 3,800 beds. It is still the largest single hospital structure in the Western Hemisphere.

In 1974, the hospital was recruiting a vice president of new Bellevue engineering, and had offered a salary of $65,000 to the ideal candidate, an engineering executive at Norwalk Hospital in Connecticut. The candidate, however, wanted $73,000 to come into the city and work for Bellevue.

210

What complicated the salary negotiations was that the city was close to bankruptcy, and all hiring had to go through the "Mac Board" controlled by Felix Rohatyn.

The candidate's salary request was denied by the board three times over four weeks. There was no way the hospital could put any additional money on any budgeted line. So in frustration, the hospital's administration paid the candidate what he asked for, $73,000.

Where did the hospital get the additional $8,000? Answer: from the Auxiliary. The candidate simply received two checks each payday, one from the city and one from the Auxiliary.

Lesson learned: When an organization, profit or non-profit, wants to hire a candidate, by hook or by crook, it will find the necessary money to complete the deal. So if you have the background, experience, and can demonstrate your **value** on paper, stick to your guns and demand what you're truly worth.

Remember, the only issue in the job market at any time is the hiring executive's problems. If the organization made you the job offer, it is saying that you're the best candidate to solve its problems. To hire someone else is to settle, or continue to leave the position vacant and continue recruitment efforts, both of which are costly. This knowledge gives you, the best candidate, a degree of leverage. Learn to use it.

Your arguments should include:

Concepts:

> It doesn't cost you to hire me, it pays! I make you money, save you money, help you get a bigger raise or promotions. I feed your wallet.

> Price is only an issue in the absence of value! If you don't believe my value, go back and review my marketing resume.

> You want to hire me with a good taste in my mouth.

Final point: Accept an appreciable cut in salary and you will spend the rest of your career trying to play catch-up financially. Better to go hungry a little longer. Also, if you accept a lower-paying job with the understanding that you would continue your job search, you will wind up with three jobs to balance: the new position, continuing family obligations, and your job search. Which one do you think is always short-changed? Yes, the job search. This is how people plateau their careers, despite their good intentions.

* * *

SAMPLE THANK-YOU LETTER

Note: This type of thank-you letter attempts to recreate the interview, and can only be prepared based on taking notes on a company's critical issues during the interview, then using the PAR method.

Thank-You Letter model

August 4, 2014

President
Company
P.O. Box 267
Monmouth, NJ 08552

Dear :

I would like to express my appreciation for the opportunity to review my extensive background and experience. I was especially pleased with the honest discussion that you and Roger provided regarding the company's immediate and future needs and opportunities. Based on our talk, I am convinced that both my background and experience at [Company Name] directly parallel your specific issues. Below is a summary of our discussion and how my background matches these issues.

Company's Issues	Steven Malone's Achievements
1. Define Business/Sales Planning Process	1. Redefined Sherwin Williams's Sales Planning Process
	a. Redefined sales planning process, which

212

shifted focus from distributor-driven/short-term to market-driven/long- and short-term. **Result**: achieved 3-year CAGR of 6.8%; almost double industry average.

2. Define Business Strategy to Pursue Key OEM Accounts Through Direct Selling

2. Conceived a Shift in Strategy From Distributor Service Reps to End-User Sales Managers.

    a. Developed job descriptions and skill sets required. Recruited experienced reps with necessary skill sets from outside the organization. Also trained existing reps to make transition. **Result**: Regional sales growth to key direct end-user accounts largest in company; Rep focus shifted from service to direct sales; Professional sales jumped 60% and industrial sales 68.5% first year.

    b. Conducted opportunity evaluation of end-user base and identified targeted accounts.

    c. Personally built long-term business relationships with targeted end-user accounts.

    d. Used event marketing to solidify business relationships, including training and entertainment.

3. Define Strategy to Increase Business With Key Distributors.

3. Developed and Implemented Strategy to Grow Existing Key Distributor Business.

    a. Partnered with Finance to identify best opportunities for revenue and profit growth. **Result**: implemented Distributor Profitability Model.

    b. Developed long-term business agreements with key distributors based on annual incremental growth. **Result**: targeted distributors' revenues grew at a rate double the average distributor.

    c. Negotiated shift from policy-based entitlements to direct management and budgeting of resources. **Result**: contribution margin increased 3.3% first year, and another 1% the second year.

4. Strengthen the Decision-Making Process Related to Business Development Resource Allocation

4. Developed a Resource Allocation Model tailored to size of opportunity, significance of market, and size of distributor. This greatly strengthened business decisions and accountability.

    a. Developed and implemented proposal process for sales initiatives.

    b. Partnered with Finance to develop a ROI model. **Result**: reduced business development spending as a percentage of sales from 4.0% to 2.9% while increasing sales 6.9% first year.

5. Restructure Sales Organization, Including Customer Service Department.

5. Directly Involved in Two Sales-Department Reorganizations.

    a. Clearly communicated benefits of new structure to Sales personnel to avoid uncertainty.

    b. Redefined employee roles, responsibilities, and decision making processes to avoid confusion and focus sale efforts. **Result**: achieved 100% subordinate buy-in; model adopted for entire sales organization.

John, I consider myself a business partner whose vision extends beyond simply the sales organization. I work well with people: internally to recruit, train and develop subordinates; and externally, to form and grow relationships with key end-users and distributors. I also consider myself an innovative problem solver. I hope the above demonstrates that the issues that presently confronts your firm are very similar to those that I have solved for [Company Name]. I am very excited about your opportunity and look forward to continuing our discussions.

Sincerely,

cc:

* * *

Client comments on the thank-you letter format:

Lloyd –

Your advice to write a long detailed thank-you note, rather than the standard two-paragraph note, sounded like a good idea. I tried it today (I kept it to two pages, not seven pages).

The recruiter liked it—see excerpt below:

"Wow, that is undoubtedly the best 'thank you' note I have seen in the 18+ years of being a recruiter. I would hire you myself after reading that! I will let you know once I have feedback."

Now we'll see if the hiring manager liked it too! I'll let you know.

Jon S.

Hey there, how are you? I wrote a thank-you to a prospective employer and forwarded a copy to the headhunter, whose comment was, "This is excellent" so… tell folks it does work!!!!

Best regards,

Nanci K.

* * *

One of the strongest trends I've seen in the last nine years is that competition for the best jobs is more intense, and the need to have additional "sales support materials" is critical. As a result, I have expanded my support for clients in this area by adding some unique materials. They include:

1. Skills Match summary. Used as interview preparation and "leave-behind" document.
2. Thank-You Letter model. Two or more pages.
3. Deal Sheet model. Used to supplement the resume and as a "leave-behind" document.
4. Best Candidate for the Job model. Interview-closing document.
5. How to Use Me model. Interview-closing document.
6. Get the Job by Doing the Job, two-page proposal. Interview-closing document.

Remember, the hiring or promotion decision usually comes down to a group of managers with their boss sitting around a conference table discussing who is the best candidate. In major-account purchasing of talent, success will go to the candidate who is *perceived* to be the best, and not to the candidate who may be the best. Therefore, how good are your sales-support materials? Are you making it easy for your "customer" to buy?

* * *

SELLING/CLOSING DOCUMENTS TO BE USED BEFORE, DURING, AND AFTER INTERVIEWS

Goal: Set yourself apart from the competition!

Tips:
Use of any of these documents will work most effectively by incorporating the PAR method.
Do not hesitate to use both regular mail and email to communicate these documents; or as "leave-behinds" after interviews.

SELLING DOCUMENTS (to be used *during* each interview)

1. LONG THANK-YOU LETTER (see above sample)

- Reconstruct the interview using the PAR method
- Length: 2-7 pages
- Note: everyone you interview with gets a thank-you letter, and *each letter must be different*

2. SKILLS MATCH SUMMARY
- Review the job description
- Compare your accomplishments vs. each of the requirements the position asks for
- Use a "T" format in your comparison; on the left side of the "T," list "JOB REQUIREMENTS" … on the right side of the "T," list "MY EXPERTISE & EXPERIENCE"
- In other words, you are matching your successes for each of the "requirements" they are asking for.
- Use as "leave-behind device"

3. DEAL SHEET (also called "Project Sheet" and "Reference Resume")
- List, in outline format, all the projects that you have worked on, and briefly describe what you did
- Very useful for: Interview preparation; for reference **during** an interview
- Use as another "leave-behind device"

CLOSING DOCUMENTS *(to be used after a second interview with the same organization)*

4. BEST CANDIDATE FOR THE JOB
- Paragraph format
- An opportunity to again communicate your business philosophy
- Can focus on your technical expertise as well as your management style

5. HOW TO USE ME
- Very useful if you're applying for a position at a lower level than your most recent experience.
- You have the opportunity here to possibly communicate to the hiring manager that you can not only do what the position you're applying for is asking, but you can also do "this, that,

and the other thing." Therefore, you can be paid what you are truly worth, and still help the hiring manager in more ways than one.

6. GET THE JOB BY DOING THE JOB

- An outline summary of what you will do during the first 12 months in the position
- Based upon:
    - Your own research of the company and its industry
    - Issues discovered and reviewed during the interview process
    - Your skills and experience geared toward helping solve identified issues
- Tell what you would do, *not how – no free consulting*

* * *

SELLING / CLOSING DOCUMENTS EXPLAINED

Objective of a Thank-You Letter

The real issue is that most people don't understand the purpose of writing a thank-you letter after an interview.

Your objective in writing a long thank-you letter after is to reconstruct, in summary format, the key issues, problems or concerns expressed by the interviewer, and how your past accomplishments have solved these types of issues.

To do this successfully, you must ask permission to take notes at the beginning of the interview. Remember also to take only brief notes during the interview; a word or two; e.g., "obsolete inventory." Your note-taking should not be a distraction. Immediately following the interview, find a convenient place to sit and expand your notes into full sentences; a bathroom, if it's raining or snowing on your car. These expanded notes will then form the basis for your long thank-you letter.

Format of a Thank-You Letter

The format of the thank-you letter is quite simple. The opening paragraph is your usual thank-you letter response. You thank the interviewer for his/her time, candor, and the useful information provided regarding the job and the company. In in my long thank-you letter approach, however, the second section is laid out in two columns using the Problem-Action-Result format. The left-hand column is a brief statement of the interviewer's problems. The right-hand column is your list of accomplishments, in Problem-Action-Result format, that matches the company's specific need or problem. You can, of course, have multiple accomplishments for each problem. As a result, the more issues or problems that you identify during the interview, the longer the thank-you letter.

In summary, a long thank-you letter achieves a number of objectives.

1. The candidate always comes across as a problem- solver or is issue-driven.
2. It recreates the basic issues discussed by the interviewer during your discussion. Thus, the candidate is able to review the business issues discussed, and provide valuable feedback and validation of the interviewer's needs and priorities. It also allows you, the candidate, to target how your accomplishments match the interviewer's current needs.

Deal Sheet

Another good way to amplify your value to an organization and take the "monkeys off the hiring executive's back" is to prepare a deal sheet. This is simply a one- or two-page summary of the various types of deals or transactions/projects you have accomplished.

Concept: the more "monkeys" you can take off of the hiring executive's back, the easier it will be for you to get hired.

Sample deal topics include M&A, divestitures, joint ventures, partnerships, alliances, long-term "blanket" agreements, leases, licensing agreements, relocations, spokesperson, etc.

Most of the time, your "deal sheet" will be used to fill a gap that appears in your resume/work history, or will simply be used as a "leave-behind device."

The "Best Candidate for the Job" Summary

This "sales" piece is very basic. A job candidate for a position is usually chosen after the key members of the hiring committee have together reviewed the paperwork on the candidates and reached a consensus. During this discussion, job candidates must to make it easy for those management committee members to argue for their candidacy. Instead of having committee members again review the details of your resume to identify critical hiring issues, such as experience with compliance issues or establishing a regional distribution center, provide them with a summary document that highlights the important elements of your resume on one to two pages. I call this document a "Best Candidate for the Job" summary.

List of Accomplishments

The summary is printed on your letterhead, and is merely a list of pertinent accomplishments that should be of interest to committee members. During the decision-making process of choosing the final candidate, those committee members who favor your candidacy can quote "chapter and verse" regarding your valuable skills and accomplishments without having to go through the verbiage in your resume. This type of "sales material" also allows you an opportunity to elaborate on qualities that are critical to the hiring decision, but not necessarily elaborated in the resume, such as leadership talent.

Examples

- **Immediate Impact:** Since I have targeted your company and know your markets, I can implement a business plan and strategies without the usual downtime. Essentially, I can come in and hit the road running.

- **Team Building and Mentoring:** In the eight years with my company, I have turned over the accounting staff three times, all internally. In each case, I have hired recent graduates and successfully trained, developed, promoted and transferred my staff to other departments.

One client of mine who used this technique related that when he closed on a senior-level position for a large financial services company, the CFO told him the "Best Candidate for the Job" summary was so effective, the CFO recommended the technique to an associate who was then "in transition."

In essence, another way to make it easy for people to hire you is to provide them with a "Best Candidate" summary that highlights those elements and qualities that may match the hiring person(s)' needs.

"Get the Job by Doing the Job" Proposal

In my approach to closing the interview process, this type of proposal or "action plan" is the strongest. Like the "Best Candidate" strategy, a job candidate needs to have had at least two separate interviews with key company executives to achieve the full value from this approach.

I first suggested this proposal technique to a Chief Information Officer with whom I was working. He'd had two interviews with a prospective company and was preparing to meet with the company's board of directors. To help close, I suggested he put together a short two-page proposal in outline format describing what he would do during the first 12 months on the job if hired.

Important point: Many professionals, when they interview with senior executives, often attempt to impress their interviewer, and wind up giving away valuable information, yet don't get hired for the position. I am a firm believer in the concept of "**no free consulting!**"

Therefore, when developing your Get the Job proposal, remember to write it as an outline *and be sure to tell your reader* what *you would do,* **not how**! In this way, if they like your proposal, they have to hire you to implement it.

Of course, you must do your homework before preparing the proposal, including researching the company, the industry, and the competition, and take good notes during your initial interviews with the company. Also, have a trusted colleague edit, proof and provide comments on your proposal before submittal to the prospective employer. By the way, when my CIO client submitted his proposal to the board of directors, the chairman commented that "he loved that I [my client] was already 'mentally in the job.'"

To sum up these two articles, it is critical, in closing the sale, that you make it **easy** for your customers to buy. Do this by:

- Using a long thank-you letter, which reconstructs your interview.
- Preparing a Best Candidate for the Job summary.
- Preparing a Deal Sheet, which summarizes the many deals/projects completed
- Preparing a Get the Job by Doing the Job proposal.

How to Evaluate *Any* Interview

The illustration below represents a typical interview.

"I" stands for interviewer and "C" stands for candidate. During the discussion, the interviewer and candidate each have a single objective, expressed by a single term:

Interviewer is **buying**!
Candidate is **selling**!

I	BUYING	TELLING & SELLING MODE
C	SELLING	BUYING MODE

If the candidate fails to make the "sale," the interviewer says, "Don't call us, we'll call you."

On the other hand, if the candidate is successful, the interview will continue, but the roles will flip. The candidate will go into a "buying mode," while the interviewer will go into a "tell and sell mode." She or he will tell you about the job, and sell you on the organization.

If you experience this "flip" during the interview, you're doing well, and will probably be asked to continue interviewing or receive a job offer.

* * *

Disappointment Letter—Sent after interview and rejection letter or phone call is received. Objective: keep the door ajar; remind the company of your continued interest.

Dear _____ :

I want to thank you for having the confidence in my candidacy to recommend that Zach Johnson and George Burton speak with me last month regarding the corporate division controller position. I am greatly disappointed that I was unsuccessful in communicating how my unique experience was perfectly suited to Brown Brothers' present and future needs.

I am convinced that my proven success at Prudential Financial with budgeting, variance analysis, measuring financial performance and cost control improvements would have quickly and appreciably added value to the Support & Control division. I really enjoy developing a core group of open-minded and aggressive individuals to improve operating efficiency.

I wish the Support & Control division at Lehman Brothers the best of luck in its selection, and would like you to know I am ready for the challenge if the successful candidate fails to achieve your expectations. I have enclosed a revised resume for future reference.

Sincerely,

Encl: resume

* * *

HOW TO PREPARE AND BETTER MANAGE
THE GROUP / PANEL INTERVIEW

I. Why companies use group interviews
    A. Spread the hiring decision risk.
    B. Save time
    C. Ultimate stress test
        1. Important to know if candidate can handle stress, especially if the job has a lot of daily stress.
        2. Convenient way to measure an applicant's mettle under fire.
        3. Identifies candidates who would work well in a group setting.
    D. Who uses group interviews?

1. Popular among academics, government agencies, nonprofits, and foreign-owned companies. Now spreading to law firms, management consultancies, and high-tech corporations.

2. Areas where they prefer decisions by consensus; reason is to reduce individual risk. Question: What does this possibly tell you about an organization?

II. Preparing for a Group Interview
   A. Get advanced notice by asking.
      1. You want to pick the brain of the recruiter by developing rapport.
   B. Information to get:
      1. Names and titles.
      2. Pecking order of panel members.
      3. Ask person setting up the interview for any inside information. Also
         a. ask former employees if they know any.
         b. check the Internet; try to demonstrate to the interview panel that you did your homework.
         c. Check out Datamonitor.com and S&P's Industry Survey.
         d. Try to obtain:
            i. The usual length of the interview.
            ii. Number of questions asked.
            iii. Key issues, then draft reply to each. Develop a cheat sheet.
   C. During the Interview:
      1. Try to look relaxed.
      2. Sit where you can maintain easy eye contact without staring toward a bright window. See Richard Fear's book: *The Stress Interview*.
      3. Show your friendliness.
         a. Shake everybody's hand with a strong handshake. Women must do this as well.
         b. Look everyone in the eye.
         c. Ask permission to take *brief* notes.
         d. Talk PAR. Consider preparing case studies ahead of time to help reduce your nervousness.
      4. Closely monitor the group's dynamics.
         a. How interviewers introduce themselves.
         b. How they talk to each other.
         c. Seating arrangements.
         d. Who leads the interview, and which person asks most of the questions?

D. After the Interview: Prepare thank-you letters to all interviewers. They must be different.

CAREER MARKETING CONSULTANTS
What Makes Recruiters Tick?
*Realizing that the search is all about **you** but the hiring process is all about **them**!*
by Jamie Feinstein

You want to work within 20 miles of your home. You want to make $65K a year. No overtime and an office with a window. OK … go for it. But to get there, you need to understand the role of recruiters and how to best maximize the relationship. The first thing you need to understand is that recruiting is a performance-based business. Many recruiters do not get a base salary! They work on a 100 percent commission basis.

You either represent a paycheck or you do not!

- If you **do**: They will call you in for an interview and/or market you to their clients.
- If you **do not**: Don't expect much … not even an acknowledgement that they are passing on you.

Don't take this personally, and don't spite yourself by writing them off. Understand that time is money to the recruiters, and they don't make any money getting back to the candidates that don't meet their criteria. If they did, they would fail. They literally have hundreds of applicant resumes a day. Instead, use it as a learning experience and a motivational tool. Ask yourself these two simple questions:

- Do I have the goods to be a viable candidate for the position?
- If I don't … why did I respond?

If you truly do "have the goods," and you did not get in the door, you can assume that your resume has failed to communicate your value. If you come to that realization, I suggest you stop focusing your time searching and applying for positions immediately! If your document is failing you, fix it! Retool the resume so that it clearly demonstrates your value. The best way to do this is to utilize the PAR methodology. (For more information: www.careermarketingforlife.com)

Recruiters are not counselors, coaches or therapists. Many may provide sound advice, but you **must** understand that they are salespeople. If they are salespeople, guess what you are!? Salespeople need products that suit the needs of their clients, and they need sales material to back it up. Get that PAR resume ASAP.

Assuming they like the product, and assuming you like the salesperson, what is next? Get in front of them and make an impact. Show up on time, dressed for success, and fill out all the required paperwork, even if it's the fifth time that day. Greet them with a firm handshake and be enthusiastic. There is an old adage in sales: "People do business with people they like." It's the little things, like a handshake, or not filling out the desired paperwork, that always rubbed me the wrong way. It's all about attitude. If the recruiter likes you as a personality, you are on your way. Some additional things to consider for the in-person meeting with a recruiter:

- Always confirm via email and/or phone
- Be prepared to wait … 15, 20, 30 minutes … keep smiling and don't cop an attitude! Fill out the required paperwork and be pleasant to the reception staff. If you are not, I promise you they will alert the recruiter to it.
- Have several copies of your resume with you.
- Be prepared to ask them questions. Ask them how their business is and what kind of year, quarter they are having. What trends are they noticing? You don't want to come across like a bump on the log. Show them that you are engaging. They want to see how you are going to present yourself to their clients.
- Tell them what you truly enjoy, but be sure to be flexible! Many recruiting firms have multiple opportunities, and may be able to present you for other positions. Be focused, but flexible.
- Don't rule out temp/consulting opportunities—keep in mind companies laid off a lot of people, but they still need to get the work done. They no longer have the budget for "permanent" employees, but many of them are bringing in temps to get the job done. Of those folks, many are getting hired. Remember: All jobs are temporary, and your next job most likely won't be your last.
- Always get an agreed-upon follow-up or next step.
- Think of ways to stay in front of them without being a pest! Gift them with articles related to their job or their clients. Refer other candidates or jobs to them. If you become an asset, you'll be kept in mind.

- A handwritten note is always a nice touch, and if you land a position through another source, a gracious letter letting them know goes a long way to maintain the relationship for future opportunities.
- **Never** "go around" the recruiter and communicate directly with the company.
- **Always** give immediate/honest feedback after you interview with one of their clients.
- Keep them in the loop and try not to surprise them at the 11th hour with another job opportunity that you're considering.

Be certain that you're prepared to accept a new position. Window-shopping with a recruiter is a big no-no! They will sniff it out and will never work with you again.

References – a word of caution! Many recruiters will ask for references, and you should oblige, but with some strict conditions. They are only to contact your references if their client has requested them. Beware that, from the recruiter's perspective, the single best source for leads is you and your references. They will call, supposedly to get a reference on you, but subtly and quickly they will turn the call into a sales call. Don't waste your references. Be careful.

* * *

References

Your references can make or break a job search. So choose them carefully and provide information on how you worked together. It makes for a more informative reference experience for the employer.

If you get an offer, and the hiring executive wants references, call your references and tell them what you've been offered, and if called, what to stress. Tutor your references!

Example:

Marietta Williams
Retired / former CFO – Wang Laboratories
Boston, MA
617-555-8888

Worked with Marietta Williams on various treasury-related projects at Wang Laboratories from 1998–2000. Assumed treasury responsibilities when she left the company in 2000.

Chapter 12

DOES AGE MATTER?

Age and savvy beats youth and skill every time.

Understand that age bias is larger in the mind of the job candidate than the hiring executive. The hiring executive's main concern is to solve their issues / problems and add VALUE to the organization.

Dealing with Prejudices on Your Resume: Age

Be careful here. Most references on resume writing advise avoiding disclosing your age on the resume. I don't subscribe to this school of thought. I believe in "full disclosure / no surprises." After all, if you are interviewing for an important position, the company will be placing a major piece of their company, namely an important area or department, in your hands. Do you really think they want surprises on your resume? I don't think so.

Don't play games on this issue. Instead, do what the famous songwriter Johnny Mercer said in one of his popular songs: "Accentuate the positive and eliminate the negative," but stick to full disclosure.

Remember, you must know the product that you're selling, because resumes don't result in jobs—interviews result in jobs. Though networking is an effective job search method, do it only *after* you've decided what your product is.

In conclusion, the issue isn't age; it's the problems employers need to solve—what's in it for them (WIIFM). If you can make money or save money for a future employer, and you can adequately communicate this fact, the self-interest of the hiring person will, in most cases, outweigh prejudice regarding age.

Concentrate your job search energy on telling your story **better**—both on paper (the marketing resume) and during the interview. The question a company wants to know today is: "Can you make a difference?" Candidates receive positions because they're expected to advance the organization's goals, solve problems, create new opportunities, and grow the business.

Final point: Spend as much time mapping your next career move as you would to planning your next overseas vacation or managing your financial portfolio.

OVERCOMING AGE BIAS: You get hired for what you can do, regardless of your age

At any age, looking for a new job can be a harrowing experience. No matter how skilled and experienced you are, the hiring process seems designed to destroy your self-esteem. How you deal with the issue of prejudice in the job market, especially age bias, can unnecessarily prolong your job search. This discussion on age bias is in two parts: concepts and practical strategies.

Part I: **Position Yourself to MinimizeAge Bias**

Most job seekers approach the issue of age bias during their job search from the wrong perspective. Usually they try to hide the issue, so they can at least get in the door, feeling that their presentation will overcome the issue. Once in the door, however, their age becomes an issue, along with the issue of full disclosure. All of a sudden, there is a surprise—your age. And most hiring executives, including executive recruiters, **hate surprises**. After all, wasn't that your motto when you ran your organization—no surprises? Hiding or running away from the age issue is the wrong way to approach the problem.

A better strategy exists: one that will allow you to overcome the issue. To begin, you must learn to continuously attack the age bias issue. Start first with the way **you** look at the issue. Remember one basic truth: the age issue is larger in your head than it is in the mind of the hiring executive. The orientation of the people who will interview you and eventually hire you is simple. Solve their problems. **Problems** are the only real issue in getting hired. Who has the problems? How can you demonstrate you're the best solution to those problems?

An article in the business section of the Sunday *New York Times* put it this way: "All businesses are looking for people who can produce more sales or profits by correcting and improving operations. Recession (or expansion) does not affect that kind of hiring. If I had applicants who would 'ring the cash register' after they came on, I would do a lot more hiring. So would others." A cover of *CFO Magazine* illustrated the issue succinctly: Creating Value: It's Your Job. As the issue's editorial points out, "only the CFO has the performance measurement tools—and the clout—to cut costs, improve operating efficiency and deploy resources carefully." A Financial Executives Networking

231

Group (FENG) member, in an email to me, recently phrased it in a very insightful way. Referring to senior financial executives, he said, "We report results, but don't sell them!" Well, if you want to overcome age bias, you'd better learn to sell.

Here are some ways to sell yourself while playing down the age issue. By the way, these tactics also apply to other types of prejudice in the job market, including sex, race, lack of specific credentials, etc., and of course, the biggest prejudice in the job market: lack of industry-specific experience.

1. **Demonstrate your value**. Job seekers 45 and older focus too much on job title, responsibilities, and the length of their experience, rather than on specific problem-solving skills and accomplishments. Show substantial accomplishments, i.e., how you were able to influence decisions by merging finance with operations for competitive advantage; how you coached the management committee into investing capital in high-return areas. But remember, you must explicitly connect your *skills* to the *needs* of the hiring manager.

   As you document your accomplishments, use the Problem-Action-Result (PAR) method to communicate these in your marketing materials **and** during the interview process. The PAR method will allow you to zero in on your accomplishments and goals, and allows you to talk about them briefly and concretely.

2. **Sucker The Reader of Your Resume**. Yes, your resume should demonstrate "full disclosure." After all, it is a contradiction to expect someone to hire you and turn over their entire operation to a person who is holding back important information. Instead, position your appreciable accomplishments in PAR format against the hiring person's personal bias. The first 95 percent of your resume presentation should answer the classic question: "What's in it for me if I hire you?" (WIIFM) Show the hiring executive that you can do the job technically, save them money, make them money, help them get a larger bonus, help them take more money to their bank. Then, at the end of your resume, you share the so-called negatives: I am 52 years old, or don't have an undergraduate degree, or whatever negative is inside your head. If you don't get the prejudice out of your head by putting it on the resume, you will always interview from a position of weakness, because of skeletons in your closet.

Bottom Line: the reason you put your weaknesses on your resume is so you can interview from a position of strength, not weakness. This approach, however, is disastrous if you fail to demonstrate your value in your resume.

Thoughts on Age Bias

You Can't Get 20 Years of Experience in a 10-Year Package. A 1985 study conducted by the outplacement firm of Challenger, Gray & Christmas found that it took people over 50 longer to get a job than it did those under 50, but then the difference was shown to be less significant. When asked why, they said it was because most of the job growth in the last five to eight years has come from very small companies. What a smaller organization wants is someone who can wear three or four hats. People over 50 are more likely to have the necessary experience.

Recognizing Strengths of Older Employees

Some years ago, ARRP had a major research organization conduct an extensive study on characteristics of older workers. In the positive area, they found older workers are admired for many important characteristics: good attendance and punctuality, commitment to quality, solid/reliable performance record, loyalty and dedication to the company, much practical—not just theoretical—knowledge, someone to count on in a crisis (recession), ability to get along with co-workers, solid experience in job and/or industry, emotional stability, and good educational background. Older workers ranked low in only three areas: physical agility, desire to get ahead, and feeling comfortable with new technologies.

In Part II of this article, we will review specific strategies to use, which will help reduce the impact of age bias.

Part II. Learn to Manage Your Image

Age is a state of mind; one you can control. And controlling that image is critical in today's competitive marketplace. Specific attitudes, actions and appearances are associated with the term "older" employee. When you know what they are, you can avoid them.

1. Learn to market yourself. It is essential to compose a 30-second commercial (elevator pitch) for yourself and then practice it at meetings and every time you're introducing yourself to others. Your pitch can also be the answer to that dreaded question: "Tell me about yourself." From my years of counseling and coaching, nothing will better improve your self-image

than developing and using a strong 30-second elevator pitch. If you can't explain what you can do **quickly**, no one will listen to you.

2. Recover from the myth that losing a job means that you have done something wrong. Also remember that anger doesn't sell; a positive attitude does.

3. Don't start off the resume summary by identifying your age. For example: I am a senior executive with more than 20 years of experience in … The reader can easily figure out that you're in your low to middle forties, if not older.

4. Under personal data, the term "grandchildren" is a dead giveaway. During the interview keep the conversation on work-related accomplishments. If asked about your personal life, mention the marathon you're training for, the mountain biking trip, and your civic and volunteer activities, like coaching youth sports.

5. Don't use worn phrases like: "At my age …", "Years ago …", "Back then …", When I was younger …", "It used to be that …", We used to …", "Listen, son …", "… up in years.", "Nowadays …", "The girls in the office …", etc. This may sound obvious, but old speech habits are often hard to break. After all, the interview is a first-person singular situation (I), yet many of us continue to use the third-person singular (We). This is a very hard shift in your speech patterns, so be careful. Put the word *"only"* before your age, if you have to say it.

6. Don't exhibit prejudice. Don't call the interviewer "honey" or "dear." Avoid calling grown women "gals" or "girls," and men as "guys" or "boys." Remember the interview is both judge and jury. So don't play into any interviewer prejudices or dislikes.

7. Don't fall technologically behind. Remember, the "old ways" aren't always bad, but they're not always the best, either. You can't afford to be perceived as not keeping your skills and knowledge up-to-date. Enroll in a software course at the local junior college. Hone your computer skills while you're in transition. You must be computer-savvy.

8. Don't mention your age. Your age is irrelevant if you're qualified for the job.

9. Don't apologize for your age. Avoid using phrases like: "You're probably looking for someone younger, but …," " "I know I'm 50, but I'm a very young 50," or "Who's going to

234

hire someone my age?" Apologizing for being 45 or older is self-deprecating, self-defeating, and plays into the prejudices that exist in the workplace. People should not be talking in terms of their age at all. Your age and experience can be a plus if you learn how to value your work and life experience.

10. Stay fit and healthy. Start slowly and build your stamina gradually. You need strength and stamina to combat the stress of finding a new position. The right wardrobe and hairstyle, and good grooming, can compensate for a less-than perfect physique. It isn't important to look young. It is important to look fit.

11. Keep your wardrobe current, but conservative. Remember, you must be able to look the part. A good book to read on this topic, even though it is dated (1988), is John T. Malloy's "Dress for Success." As for hairstyle, keep it simple, attractive and conservative. Don't use your kid's barber. Get your hair stylized. An impressive watch, expensive shoes, and attaché case are an interview necessity for both men and women. If your old attaché case is scuffed and shabby, treat yourself to a new one.

12. Get rid of the job-security notion. Each person needs to look at him- or herself as being self-employed. All jobs are temporary, so keep up with your field.

Make sure that your habits, attitudes, and outward appearances are in step with what is accepted in the business world. If you are shooting for a position paying six figures, you better look like you're worth that kind of money.

Turn Age to Your Advantage.

The following editorial appeared in *Business Marketing* magazine: "Get me an Old Pro Fast. As the economic seas grow rougher and rougher, I've noticed the hotshot younger set is increasingly looking to Old Pros. It's an almost instinctual reflex. The Old Pros have been there before. Or, put another way: In an up market, most anybody with lots of energy can make some money. But in a shaky, downward-spiraling market, success frequently depends on a combination of a lot of energy plus plenty of moxie borne of experience."

When you sense that age is an issue, go on the offense. The best way to answer age-related questions that come up in an interview is to be prepared for them and not get caught off guard. One client I worked with was asked a series of questions that indicated the interviewer wanted to know her age.

She responded by saying: "I think what you're asking me is 'How long will I be in this position?' Then she paused and said firmly, in a style that demonstrated her keen negotiating skills, "I'm committed to be at your company at least five years. How many younger candidates can promise you that?"

Then there's the sincere approach: "I'm 55. (But continue your response, which has been prepared ahead of time and memorized). I'm in excellent health, and, as you can see from my resume, I have an impressive record of experience and achievement to contribute. I plan to be making a contribution for a good, long time."

* * *

Rallying the Troops

If you've been diligent, completed the exercises, internalized the marketing and sales concepts, and produced a marketing resume that answers the three critical hiring questions, then you're ready to take on the world. Since perception rules over reality, the cards are now stacked in your favor.

Good Luck!

Lloyd Feinstein
Career Marketing Consultants
25 Dawson Lane
Monroe, New Jersey 08831

www.careermarketingforlife.com
LloydFeinstein@yahoo.com
609.655.7300 Office

* * *

End Note

The author has been operating a **career marketing** and **advisory service** in the New York City metropolitan area for more than 28 years. To learn more about his services, visit his website (www.careermarketingforlife.com), YouTube (http://vimeo.com/11797338), and LinkedIn site (https://www.linkedin.com/pub/lloyd-feinstein/0/747/584). In addition, he welcomes comments on the book series, as well as inquiries regarding his counseling services. Direct inquiries to:

Lloyd Feinstein
Career Marketing Consultants
25 Dawson Lane
Monroe, New Jersey 08831

www.careermarketingforlife.com
LloydFeinstein@yahoo.com
609.655.7730 Office

ACKNOWLEDGMENTS

I prevailed upon my clients and friends to critique various drafts of the manuscript. They agreed and *Shorten Your Job Search* is greatly improved as a result. Many thanks to Linda Kline, my coauthor on a previous career book; Barbara Haislip, Andy O'Hearn, Shim Mordzynski, and Sanford Werfel. Jack Quinn gave his time and thoughts, along with an article, to the project. Thanks. Annemarie Cocchia provided invaluable insight, and Ed Wexler provided illustrations (one of the best caricature artists working in print today). Thank you all for your valuable assistance. In addition, I owe much gratitude to the Somerset Hills YMCA in Basking Ridge, New Jersey for sponsoring a job search support group (Career Forum) for the past 21 years. It was here that I was able to test my unconventional strategies and ideas that form a major part of this book. Also, a big thanks to my co-chairpersons at the Forum, Denis Dooley and Robert Stomber. I owe thanks most of all, though, to my wife Joan. None of this would have been possible without her love and support over the past 28 years while I conducted my career counseling practice from a home office. And I would like to thank my two sons, Keith and Jamie, for their support and encouragement through the years. Thanks, guys!

CONTINUE TO STRENGTHEN YOUR CAREER MANAGEMENT SKILLS

SHORTEN YOUR JOB SEARCH
Build Confidence, Communicate Your Value and Quickly Land Your New Job!

Book One: Constructing the Marketing Resume

CONTENTS

Introduction

Chapter 1: The Hiring Process.
Understanding it. Who hiring managers want. How to stand out from the crowd by showing your value and your fit.

Chapter 2: Key Factors in Managing Your Career.
The importance of perception, the sales nature of any job search, and how your presentation totally influences it. A manager's view of the hiring model.

Chapter 3: How Do I Get Familiar with the Marketing Resume?
What's a Marketing Resume? Is that different from my current one?
How the "Marketing Resume" and the weaknesses of traditional resumes are reviewed. Resume importance, role in the hiring process, and the need for your resume to answer any hiring executives' three critical issues: Are you able to do the job? Do you have the right experience solving their problems? and Will you fit in?

Chapter 4: Learn How Storytelling Can Better Communicate Your Value. Would you show yourself to your interviewer in action, sound and color?
This chapter demonstrates in detail how storytelling is the most effective communication technique in the resume, the job hunt, and on the job.

Chapter 5: Define Your Management and Personality Style.
You're a fly-on-the-wall watching yourself do business, as well as your personal life.
How to include your personality on the resume—it's 90 percent of the hiring decision. Detailed instruction is given in the use of 360° feedback on achieving this important step.

Chapter 6: Marketing Resume Construction: A Step-by-Step Approach

*You are instructed how to best define yourself using less than six words. How to define your skill set (areas of expertise) in great detail (i.e., **process**, the first of only two transferable skills which require no further written verification).*

Chapter 7: How to Describe Your Experience: Storytelling.

How to communicate your value and compete are discussed in detail with before-and-after examples. A back-and-forth conversation develops a typical storytelling (Problem-Action-Result) paragraph. Storytelling examples (PARs) in 27 common job categories.

Chapter 8: Connecting the Dots to Create a Marketing Resume.

Creating the Marketing Resume. The elements include contact information, personality / management style, skill set / areas of expertise, work history in Problem-Action-Result format, education, affiliations, personal data and interests. Marketing Resume examples are provided, with an extensive list of resume writing tips.

Chapter 9: Strengthen the Mechanics of Your Job Search by Taking the Show on the Road.

Using your Marketing Resume, special emphasis is given on how to answering ads, work with employment agencies and executive search firms, and network. How to develop a two-minute pitch, targeting recruiters, how to network, and how to use direct-mail strategies to capture the "hidden" job market.

APPENDIX

REFERENCES / BIBLIOGRAPHY / NOTES

Links of Interest:

Recruiters: *The Recruiting & Search Report*, P.O. Box 9433, Panama City Beach, Florida 32417; 850.235.3733; www.rsronline.com. Best source for both retained executive search (headhunters) and contingency recruiters (employment agencies).

Articles:

Fraser, J. A. "Disguising the Signs of Being 'Outplaced'." New York Times [New York, NY] 24 Sept. 1994, The Executive Life Column sec.: n. pag. New York Times. Web. 20 Apr. 2015. <http://www.nytimes.com/1994/10/23/business/l-choose-your-outplacement-wisely-611883.html>.

Hamel, Gary. "Strategy as Revolution." *Harvard Business Review*. Harvard Business Review, July-Aug. 1996. Web. 20 Apr. 2015. <https://hbr.org/archive-toc/3964?cm_sp=Article-_-Links-_-Magazine+Issue>.

Kotter, John. "The Power of Stories." *Forbes*. Forbes Magazine, 12 Apr. 2006. Web. 20 Apr. 2015. <http://www.forbes.com/2006/04/12/power-of-stories-oped-cx_jk_0412kotter.html>.

Tavris, Carol. "You Are What You Do: The Freedom to Change." *Prime Time* (1980): n. pag. Print. November 1980.

Waldroop, James, and Timothy Butler. "Finding The Job You SHOULD Want." *Forbes*, 2 Mar. 1998. Web. 20 Apr. 2015. <http://archive.fortune.com/magazines/fortune/fortune_archive/1998/03/02/238545/index.htm>. *Each year, students at the Harvard Business School take a quiz to help find a career in which they'll flourish and be happy. Here's a short-form version.*

Webb, Chadd. "Strategies and Techniques for Positioning Yourself in the Competitive Job Market." *DVD Review* (n.d.): n. pag. *Co-Editor/ Movie Zone.*

Webber, Alan M. "Is Your Job Your Calling (extended Interview)." *Fast Company*. N.p., 31 Jan. 1998. Web. 20 Apr. 2015. <http://www.fastcompany.com/33545/your-job-your-calling-extended-interview>. February-March, 1998.

Visuals:

Ed Wexler Illustrations: http://www.g7animation.com/G7/Ed_Wexler.html

Lloyd Feinstein on Vimeo/YouTube: http://vimeo.com/11797338 and https://www.youtube.com/watch?v=QDbG2gdpSMU

Lloyd Feinstein on YouTube *(dual DVD)*: https://www.youtube.com/watch?v=QZqL7lBsgc0 (Part I) and https://www.youtube.com/watch?v=1OaSmOhsn2o (Part II)

Keith Feinstein: Creative Director, Media Contact, Eureka Exhibits: keith@eurekaexhibits.com; 1-908-644-8373; http://www.eurekaexhibits.com/about-us/team/

Books:

Boll, Carl, *Executive Jobs Unlimited*, Macmillan, 1965. http://www.amazon.com/Executive-Jobs-Unlimited-Carl-Boll/dp/002512790X *(Direct Mail)*

Borden, Richard C., *Public Speaking—As Listeners Like It!*, Harper & Row, 1935. http://www.amazon.com/Public-Speaking-As-Listeners-Like/dp/B000857Q90 *(Direct Mail)*

Drucker, Peter F., *The Effective Executive*, HarperBusiness Essentials, 1967. http://www.amazon.com/The-Effective-Executive-Definitive-Harperbusiness/dp/0060833459

Feinstein, Lloyd, and Kline, Linda, *Career Changing: The Worry-Free Guide*, Little, Brown and Company, 1982. http://www.amazon.com/Career-Changing-Worry-Free-Guide/dp/0316498580 *(Overview)*

Feinstein, Lloyd L., *Shorten Your Job Search: Build Confidence, Communicate Your Value and Quickly Land Your New Job* (Book One: Constructing the Marketing Resume), Career Marketing Consultants, Monroe, N.J., 2015. http://www.amazon.com/Shorten-Your-Job-Search-Communicate/dp/0991588207

Harrigan, Betty, *Games Mother Never Taught You: Corporate Gamesmanship For Women*, Warner Books, 1981. http://www.amazon.com/Games-Mother-Never-Taught-You/dp/0892560193

Johnson, Barbara L., *Private Consulting: How to Turn Experience into Employment Dollars*, Prentice-Hall, Inc., 1982. http://www.alibris.com/Private-Consulting-How-to-Turn-Experience-Into-Employment-Dollars-Barbara-L-Johnson/book/5347716 *(Going into Your Own Business)*

Ogilvy, David, *Confessions of an Advertising Man*, Dell Publishing, 1963. http://www.amazon.com/Confessions-Advertising-Man-David-Ogilvy/dp/190491537X

Rackham, Neil, *SPIN Selling (Situation–Problem–Implication–Need/Payoff)*, McGraw-Hill Book Company, 1988. http://www.amazon.com/SPIN-Selling-Neil-Rackham/dp/0070511136 *(Selling Yourself to Others)*

Tarrant, John, *Perks and Parachutes: Negotiating Your Executive Employment Contract*, Linden Press/Simon & Schuster, 1985. http://www.amazon.com/Perks-parachutes-negotiating-executive-employment/dp/B001VUU8AK *(Salary Negotiations)*

* * *

HOW TO NEGOTIATE AN OUTPLACEMENT AGREEMENT and SELECT A COUNSELING FIRM: Timing Is Everything!

As with all negotiations, you want to do it from a position of strength, not weakness. Since you have little or no leverage once an organization lets you go, that is not the best time to negotiate an outplacement agreement. Instead, *before* you join a company is proper time to get your employer to agree to an outplacement agreement. Since the company wants to "close" the sale and get you on board, and because it doesn't cost the company anything at the time to agree to an outplacement provision, this is the most opportune time to negotiate your outplacement. Of course, it should be a written employment agreement (either formal contract or informal letter of agreement).

Negotiating for outplacement services *during* the hiring process requires little additional effort, just determination. An outplacement provision in your employment agreement must be a non-negotiable item, because if you are let go, salary continuation and outplacement assistance are the two most critical elements. One allows you to pay your financial obligations, and the other allows you to find a new position more quickly, thus preserving a majority of your severance pay.

In your employment agreement, key outplacement issues to include: (a) a set fee amount for outplacement services, usually 10 to 15 percent of an employee's base annual cash compensation; (b) outplacement services provided by a firm of the employee's choosing, *not* the company's. That may mean you need to investigate firms outside of the two or three recommended by the company. Remember, any company that fires you should not be allowed to choose your doctor, lawyer or outplacement service. They cannot be counted on to have your best interests at heart.

How do you evaluate an outplacement service? The list below details some of the key questions you should ask when assessing an outplacement firm.

1. What is the firm's approach to individual outplacement? Does it represent a conceptual whole, or is it just loose concepts? Note: Tactical energy, in a strategic and conceptual void, is a recipe for disaster (Madeleine Albright).
2. What industries/markets/functions/levels does the firm/counselor specialize in, if any?
3. What are the professional credentials of the firm, and most importantly, those of its staff counselors—especially the counselor with whom you will work? What is the counselor's caseload? An appropriate number is 10 to 20.
4. Since time is always limited in outplacement counseling, how are participants provided with individual instruction/counseling? Office vs. cubicle? For the dollars spent, what specific

services are provided? Ask for details about computers, databases, private phone lines. Can you get this in writing?

5. What is the firm's success rate? Describe any failures the firm has had. Will the firm allow you to speak with previous clients, both satisfied and dissatisfied?

6. Do participants have the opportunity to develop customized targeted resumes and cover letters?

7. Who will actually be your career advisor and coach? What are his or her business credentials? May I meet with him or her? What is the advisor's philosophy of counseling?

8. How is the critical issue of a client's self-assessment handled?

9. Are there structured group experiences where clients can share experiences? What is the atmosphere of the office, i.e., positive or depressing?

10. What experience does the counselor/advisor have in working with employees in your industry? Ask for references. You should talk with someone from your industry who has been through the program.

11. What is the firm's track record working with women? Minorities? All levels? Early retirement situations?

12. What qualities make your firm better than other outplacement counseling firms? What percentage of your firm's business is group outplacement vs. individual executive outplacement?

Should you have to negotiate an outplacement agreement after you have been terminated from your job, the negotiation process becomes more tenuous and difficult. Nevertheless, some strategies and techniques can improve your chances for success.

First, try to negotiate with the person who has the greatest feelings of guilt regarding your situation. This usually is the person who fired you; i.e., your boss. You do have one thing on your side. The company will probably want you to sign an agreement not to sue. Do not sign anything until you have negotiated everything you can. You must work the guilt angle. Explain to your boss how difficult the job search will be in your industry and/or functional discipline. Use the data from national publications like the *Wall Street Journal* and other business information sources you can research. Also emphasize to your boss, however, that it is in his/her and the organization's best interest to provide you with an equitable severance package, including outplacement services. Your argument is simple: you are trying to be kept whole, not attempting to enrich yourself at the organization's expense. Also understand that you can negotiate a second, though smaller outplacement assignment, if the first firm failed to meet your expectations.

Point out to your boss what's in it for the company. Specifically, cover the following points: (a) You will be a good soldier—not bad-mouth the company. (b) You will be available to consult, if necessary, on current projects; free, if of short duration (one day); paid, if of long duration. (c) You will be a ready resource via the telephone regarding past company / department issues.

Final thought: Nobody will give you anything; you have to ask for it. Be persistent and ask for what you want. You should always demand to have the important benefits of a professional outplacement counselor. At work, you hired the best consultants. Do the same for your most important assignment—your career.

HOMEWORK ASSIGNMENT SUPPORT MATERIALS

Handouts That Support the DVD on YouTube

1. DVD Review

"Strategies and Techniques for Positioning Yourself in the Competitive Job Market," DVD review written by Chad Webb, Movie Zone editor for pop culture site 411mania.com http://411mania.com/movies/category/reviews/

Let's face it, seminars can be boring. You sit in a room and listen to someone lecture or talk for hours with PowerPoint presentations, charts, and graphs. It can be tiring and uninspiring, to say the least. What sets the good ones and the bad ones apart is the topic. Lloyd Feinstein's seminar is so wonderfully different and the opposite of dreary because he is discussing résumés and interviewing, two subjects that are always vital and important to the public. Mr. Feinstein takes everything we have learned about submitting a résumé, and turns it upside down. The result is an informative and startling education on how to better our situation in life.

Over the course of approximately three-and-a-half hours, Feinstein unveils aspects of how he repackages his clients so that their résumés reflect what the hiring executive wants. He has been a seasoned career counselor for many years, and has boosted the lives of more than 2,700 executives and professionals. His seminar is entitled *Strategies and Techniques for Positioning Yourself in the Competitive Job Market*, and was taped in Rockefeller Center in New York City in June 2007. Feinstein's style is unique, challenging, and exciting, because many of his lessons are contrary to what we have read and been taught in school. He explains this fact right away, and urges the audience to ask questions whenever they disagree. In front of a group of around 25 people, he gradually changes the way in which normal business people think. His methods have been printed for articles in the *Wall Street Journal*, and he constantly aids in assisting all sorts of clients to further their careers.

Unless you are in college or younger, admitting that you need help in constructing a résumé is not easy. I know this because I was faced with the problem of transferring job fields. After making the mistake of choosing a major that did not fit my interests, I was met with a hurdle of trying to get my foot in the door of a profession in which I had little experience. Working with Lloyd Feinstein has been invigorating and stimulating. Acknowledging that someone else can assist in molding your job history into appearing attractive for potential hiring executives was difficult, but ultimately effective.

Feinstein's key strategies greet viewers as the DVD begins, and then the seminar starts. Before leaping into the meat of the discussion, he asks everyone to get out their business cards and place them next to his. He subsequently requests that they turn the cards over. He points out that they have stopped selling themselves because nothing was printed on the back, whereas his own had more details visible on the back of the card. The goal was to get the room's attention, and that mission was accomplished. This display makes one ruminate intensely about how they present themselves to others.

When a résumé is afforded to a hiring manager, you only have 10 seconds of their time. This is a tip that Feinstein stresses and reiterates throughout his presentation, and it might be the most important one. This makes the task of shaping an eye-catching document more demanding, but the payoff is certainly worth it in the end. Feinstein divulges numerous facets of his approach to interviewing and resumes, but he never exposes an excessive amount. After all, he is selling this to his audience, and by the persistent questions and discussions on the topics, it is obvious that his message is leaving an earnest impression.

As the population grows, the amount of people with special circumstances regarding their aspiring careers continues to increase. As time goes on, it seems as if the positions the majority of the public end up adopting is not what they truly want to do. Lloyd Feinstein offers a chance to embrace that dream, and at the very least give it a valiant effort before retreating to the familiar. Some of his figures land as difficult to accept. For instance, his audience immediately responded to the fact that only around 4 percent to 5 percent of jobs are filled through use of the internet. As a culture, we rely on computers and the web, but to obtain a valuable position, the internet is not the wise means to pursue it. Taking extra time to research library materials or skim the newspaper can work wonders.

He stands in front of the group with the utmost confidence. Feinstein is always in control of the conversation and never hesitates to defend a comment. He examines several résumés out loud and addresses what is wrong with them and how they should be altered. He also discloses the technique of PAR, which is applying a problem, an action, and a result to accomplishments from your work history. Knowing that human resources is the enemy, acknowledging that a résumé is considered a risk-reduction document to an employer, revealing a full disclosure of your past, and understanding how to sell and close the interview process, are all crucial items that Lloyd expresses.

The room in which his seminar takes place exudes an intimate atmosphere, and that is essential, because if his approach is to appear convincing and indispensable, then the speaker must converse on a down-to-earth level, and Feinstein does. The picture quality of the DVD is startlingly excellent, with very little grain or jumpy spots in the camera movements. The sound is commendable, aside from some soft-talking audience members and extremely loud sirens outside. Overall, the quality of the technical specifications is consummate.

After Feinstein is finished promoting his innovative and brave system of career revitalization, it seems foolish that we did not adopt this practice before. He unravels his presentation as being a highway to the happiness and comfort that everyone deserves. During his time, he uses many quotes to ingrain certain points. One of them conveys that the hardest part is discounting the habitual ways to which we have become accustomed, not learning the new. Absorbing Mr. Feinstein's tactics is not a walk in the park. It takes determination, fortitude, and concentration, but I was always taught that things will get more grueling before they get better.

* * *

Hello:

I completed a two-part seminar for the on-line site 6FigureJobs.com. It was held in a large law conference room in Rockefeller Center, New York City. I took advantage of the opportunity to record my presentation, and since each part was over an hour in length, I had it converted into a dual DVD. Then, to make the information easily accessible, I had the DVDs "broken" down into key segments by running time. For your benefit, I have provided these presentations, and I hope you find them useful and enjoyable.

–Lloyd Feinstein

* * *

Here are links to the comprehensive video. It is in two parts. The combined presentation is two hours and 41 minutes long.

This will open into Part I in your YouTube page on your browser.

https://www.youtube.com/watch?v=QZqL7lBsgc0 *(1:14:08 running time)*

Below is a table of contents for Parts I & II of the video.

Strategies & Techniques for Positioning Yourself in the Competitive Job Market
by Lloyd Feinstein
http://www.careermarketingforlife.com

All start times are given in (Hour:Minutes:Second) format (H:MM:SS)

Part 1 of 2: http://www.youtube.com/watch?v=QZqL7lBsgc0

Part 2 of 2: http://www.youtube.com/watch?v=1OaSmOhsn2o *(1:27:04 running time)*

The Interviewing Model (1:16:05)
Wrap-Up and Summary (1:22:36)

* * *

The indexing of topics with the correct time slots will make it convenient to refresh any my concepts and methods.

For those who have not viewed the video previously, and only saw me in the classroom, the two parts should prove very helpful and thought-provoking (see client comments below).

When viewing the video it is helpful to watch with a friend or colleague, so when you explain an idea, it helps you strengthen your own understanding.

Also provided is a review of the video that was written by Chad Webb, Movie Zone editor for pop culture site 411mania.com.

Support materials for the video are below, and include the necessary handouts used during the presentation, the blog movie write-up, and client comments.

* * *

Wishing you smart career management,

Regards,
Lloyd

www.careermarketingforlife.com
LloydFeinstein@yahoo.com
609.655.7730 Office

* * *

CLIENT COMMENTS ON THE DVD

"I am looking at the DVD—it is simply fascinating! Will stay tuned. Suddenly the job search has become an enjoyable experience."
–P. C., Manager, New Product Development and Innovation

"I got a great deal from the DVD. I'll watch it a second time to reinforce what I saw first time."
–C. W., Organization Development (OD) Consultant

"The information you gave and shared with me is invaluable, especially the DVD. After reviewing it, I would like to add a couple of jobs that I left off my drafted resume so that there are no surprises. In addition, I really need your help in thinking and writing in process format in a concise way. I have trouble here. Thank you for your continued help and I look forward to talking and meeting with you again very soon."
–R.J., Marketing Consultant

"The video was a great presentation of all that you have taught in past presentations that I have attended. It was well-paced and the quality was very good. I learned more about the process each time I see it presented."
–S.C., IT Consultant

* * *

POSITIONING YOURSELF IN A DIFFICULT JOB MARKET

with Lloyd Feinstein

New York City
June 8, 2013
8 a.m. to Noon

***

A COMPETITIVE ADVANTAGE

Background: Below are the results of an analysis of 210 resumes on Logistics/Materials Management professionals whose documents were distributed by their trade association, The Council of Logistics Management.

Source: Craig Wanggaard

ANALYSIS FACTORS

Analysis Factors	#	%
Right-justified	118	56
Personality Characteristics	5	2
Different Font Styles	49	23
PAR Paragraphs	0	0
Areas of Expertise	20	9.5
Military Experience	39	18.5
Master's Degree	70	33

Conclusion: Most everyone prepares their resume the wrong way.

JOB SEARCH MODEL

FIVE-STEP JOB SEARCH MODEL

Step I. Product Analysis / Self-Assessment (most important)

A. Packaging Yourself—PAR Method

B. Homework Assignment

Step II. Determine Employer's Needs

A. Want-Ad Analysis

Step III. Develop Marketing Materials

A. Targeted Resume

B. Action / Marketing Letters

C. Case Study

D. Core Competencies

E. Other Communications Pieces

1. Thank-You Letters-2-7 pages

2. Disappointment Letters

3. Proposals

Step IV. Campaign Mechanics

A. Want-Ad Advertisements

B. Executive Search Firms and Employment Agencies

C. "Hidden" Job Market

D. Networking

1. Written Networking Approach

Step V. The Interview

A. Interviewing Backward—A Practical Strategy

B. Activities Before, During and After the Interview

C. Evaluating Your Performance in the Interview.

MATERIALS TO SUPPORT THE PERSONALITY DESCRIPTION

List #1—Describe Yourself

From: (Cover Letter)
Date:
To:

Subject: Career Counseling—updated
Attachments: There is 1 attachment

Dear _____:

I am taking the time and effort to develop a new targeted resume and am using a new book entitled "The World's Greatest Resume."

As part of the book's counseling process, I need to gather input from people I have worked with to formulate my revised resume.

I would appreciate your participation. Specifically, please review and complete the bottom of this page and the next pages, then email them back to my assistant. The information will be totally confidential.

On this page, please review the business processes listed under Areas of Expertise. First, do you agree with the Areas of Expertise? Second, can you think of anything I should add, delete or change from the list of business processes?

Thank you so much for your help!

Sincerely,

Phone/Email

Areas of Expertise

1.

2.

3.

4.

5.

6.

* * *

List #2—Describe Yourself

Name: _____

From:_____ Date: _____

To improve my resume and other marketing materials, could you please spend a few minutes **checking off the 10 adjectives** that you feel accurately describe how I functioned on the job? Then, please double XX the one adjective of the 10 which best describes me. Your answers will remain confidential by sending your results directly to _____. Email your response as a Word document. (Note: Please save your responses before you email.)

Seasoned		Organized	
Diligent		Confident	
Technically oriented		Bright	
Flexible		Quietly assertive	
Loyal		Versatile	
Decisive		Profit-oriented	
Resourceful		Consistent	
Analytical		Responsive	
Team Player		Persistent	
Results-oriented		Persuasive	
Competitive		Ambitious	
Goal-Oriented		Insightful	
Energetic		Efficient	
Tough-minded		Precise	

	Cost-conscious		Driven
	Hands-on		Self-Starter
	Dedicated		Pragmatic
	Financially oriented		Cost-effective
	Enthusiastic		Project-oriented
	Resilient		

Check all the phrases that apply, and feel free to add your own.

	Accustomed to handling multiple assignments
	Excels under pressure
	Gets the job done
	Meets the priorities and deadlines
	Creative problem-solver
	Used to a fast pace
	Adjusts easily to emergencies
	At ease delivering presentations and public speaking
	Excellent writer

Please identify one thing that you think this person does particularly well.
Thank you for your help.

* * *

List #3—Accomplishments

SAMPLE AREAS OF EXPERTISE BY JOB CATEGORY

ACCOUNTING

Cash & Working Capital Management, including cash flow forecasting, cash collection, minimizing cash expenditures, vendor relations & negotiations, cash controls, and inventory management.

ADVERTISING & PUBLIC RELATIONS

Account Management Supervision, including hiring, training, motivating, coaching, directing/focusing account directors and account executives, goals settings and targets, account planning (strategic and tactical), identifying client requirements, establishing the account management policies and political aspects of the clients' accounts, contract negotiations, account team compensation, planning and recognition, forecasting, measurement systems and sales tracking.

Public Relations, including strategic plan development, media relations, national media placement, analyst relations, crisis communications, community relations, product publicity, new product introductions, trade show support, special events, spokesperson tours, news conferences, annual reports, spokesperson briefings, writing news, creating and placing features, and scripting and producing VNR and ANRs.

ANALYTICS

Economic/Quantitative Analysis, including global economics and market trends, econometrics and statistical based analysis and forecasting, attribution and risk analysis, portfolio/performance analysis, database building and management, and compliant performance reporting.

AUDITING

Value-Added Internal Auditing (operational/EDP/compliance/system pre-implementation) , including risk assessment, audit planning, researching business processes and identifying common risks, audit analysis, evaluating control processes to mitigate business risk and executive reporting.

BANKING

Risk Assessment & Credit Analysis, including balanced assessment of client's key business and financial risks, audit financial statements; reviewing management letters, external research reports, prospectus, industry publications, and regulatory reports; supplemented with due diligence calls to customer, identifying relevant credit issues and recommending specific actions to mitigate open issues.

BENEFITS

Risk & Employee Benefit Plans, including risk analysis, benefits planning & design, identifying carriers and negotiating funding strategies, forecasting costs, executive presentations and consensus building, benefit rollout, employee communications, documentation and compliance, and daily administration.

BROKERAGE

Trading/Portfolio Management, including managing a market making options book composed of treasury bonds, futures and listed options, swaps, swaptions, caps/floors, eurodollar futures and options, as well as structured transactions under the "least cost hedge" principle. Continuous monitoring of market developments and evaluation of strategic trading positions. Preparation of daily report of P/L and cost of carry for senior management. **Electronic Trading**: Bloomberg, Reuters, Telerate, Excel, MS Word, Eurex (DTB), Cantor e-speed, Globex/Project A, Windows NT and Solaris.

BUSINESS DEVELOPMENT

Strategic Business Development of multinational and multifaceted programs, including defining corporate direction, long- and short-term business planning, market analysis and segmentation, customer requirement identification, determining growth strategies, implementation of strategic plans via acquisition or development of new businesses, logistical and distribution operations, marketing and sales proposal development, and brand repositioning.

CONSULTING

Operations Consulting, including scoping and pricing of engagements, proposal development, conducting in-depth organizational and operations reviews, develop findings and recommendations, developing financial forecast models to quantifying impact of recommendations, reports to "C"-level management, managing engagement budgets, supervising and evaluating staff, and closing engagements.

ENGINEERING

Project Engineering, Product & Process Development from project proposal through production, including contract review, Statement of Work (SOW) and scope of objectives, identify existing products and/or modifications to meet the customer's needs, identifying internal requirements, electronic hardware design tasks, specifications development, costs and schedule quoting, internal and customer design reviews, final implementation of sub-system (circuit card assembly) and system quality assurance verification and validation testing.

EVENTS MANAGEMENT

Special Events Management from inception through completion, including developing work breakdown structures, monitoring costs against budgets; selection of vendors, venues and services; program tracking against schedules, contingency planning, daily project supervision, conducting project status meeting, follow-up and documentation.

EXECUTIVE ASSISTANT

Administrative Support to senior executive, including bonus plan management, public relations (compliant resolution, trade association relations, writing and editing newsletter), coordinating departmental relocation, telecommunications, purchasing, expense accounting, preparation of travel accommodation, and producing manuscripts. Skills include (80 wpm), machine transcription, Microsoft Office 2013, Microsoft Outlook, Internet, HTML, PowerPoint (animated slides), and Meeting Maker.

FINANCIAL

Financial Operations Management, including budgeting & forecasting, analysis, controllership, cost accounting (standard, job order, process, direct), long term contract accounting, legal, audit, tax planning & compliance, cost-reduction programs, and using the latest computer programs.

FINANCIAL RISK MANAGEMENT

Financial Risk Management, including frameworks to assess financial risk and models to measure risk; execution of both interest rate and foreign exchange strategies on global basis using swaps, options, FRAs and forwards; knowledge of international hedging markets; refinement of hedging strategies in light of new Accounting Standards (FAS 133 and FAS 138); development of ISDA master contracts, development and oversight of treasury risk systems; and oversight of classic insurance risk.

GENERAL MANAGEMENT

General Management, including full P&L responsibility, vision definition and communication, forecasting and budgeting, line management & control, business-plan development, resource allocation and asset management, business structure process and design, performance management, organization development & succession planning, talent evaluation & team building, management & staff training, and CEO-to-CEO solution selling.

HUMAN RESOURCES

Human Resources Management, including talent acquisition, retention and termination; leadership identification and development, succession planning, benefits, compensation and rewards, performance management, career development, relations with union and non-union workforce, and diversity.

INSURANCE

Property/Casualty Insurance Underwriting, including creating opportunities to pursue new business leads, gathering data, researching information about risks under consideration, negotiating coverage terms and pricing, developing combinations of price and coverage to satisfy both client and company, and profitable underwriting through effectively selecting and pricing individual risks and accounts.

INTERNATIONAL

Domestic/International Working Capital Management, including product pricing, sales terms, customer credit analysis, A/R collections, off-balance sheet receivables financing, and payments netting among domestic and offshore legal entities.

INTERNET

IT Documentation, Web and Online Help Projects from inception to delivery, including identifying user needs, defining deliverables, integrating customer feedback, scheduling, designing, developing and maintaining deliverables, integrating customer feedback, scheduling, designing, developing and maintaining deliverables, development schedules and budgets. Windows and web-based Help, work closely with system developers to identify development platform, set web standards and styles, integrate page level and comprehensive Help with system IT supports.

LEGAL

Intellectual Property, including research and analysis of client needs; knowledge of current law; evaluation of client IP portfolio; preparation and prosecution of patent, trademark and copyright applications; preparation and issuance of opinions of patentability, non-infringement and validity; and, reviewing and researching competitor's IP.

LOGISTICS / PURCHASING

Contract/Proposal Management, including follow-up with customers, and as well as reviewing existing contracts as they get close to term, analyzing current business environment and company needs, renewing/renegotiating as required, evaluation of RFP/RFI, risk/opportunity analysis, identifying and soliciting stakeholder input, formation of proposal strategy, development of compliance matrix, facilitating review meetings, gap analysis and solution requirements, writing and submitting contract/proposal, vendor evaluation and acceptance selection, and contract negotiations, both short- and long term-blanket purchase agreements, price, terms, quality and delivery.

MARKETING

Market & Strategic Business Analysis, including analyzing and identifying current and emerging trends in business, lifestyle, design and technology; identifying new or alternative product ideas, technology policy and investments, manufacturing locations, marketing strategies or channels of distribution; communicating the analysis and making recommendations to clients and/or senior management.

MEDICAL

Clinical Research & Drug Development, including development of clinical plan with regulatory strategy (Phase I-III), design and development of clinical protocols with IRB submission, regulatory submission, study conduct, DMC review, CSRs, conference abstracts and manuscripts for publication, data evaluation against Go/No-Go criteria, IND writing, and presentation of results to management, scientific and regulatory audiences.

MERGERS & ACQUISITIONS

M&A Structuring & Execution (Domestic & International) with transaction origination, concept justification and introductory meetings, valuation and other analyses, testing and building of partnerships and planning for necessary disposals, structuring & negotiating terms, and final documentation and closing.

NONPROFIT

Nonfinancial and Not-for-profit Management (501(c)(3) organizations) , including overseeing Executive Directors and advising on ED's direction of staff and all operations, applying financial management and performance driven accountability to strengthen missions; applying private equity and financial disciplines to fiscal management. Also, handle board strengthening, updating governance and regulatory and legal compliance, establishing committees, and delegating work functions. Oversee capacity building for replication and scaling up of public health programs, motivating and directing volunteers, promoting advocacy, fundraising, program development, marketing and public relations.

OPERATIONS

Operations Management & Supervision, including preparing & scheduling work flow; laboratory support & preparation of all materials, media and equipment for labs and field courses; documentation and recording for future reference and use, inventory and maintenance of equipment and supplies, care of all live materials, government compliance, liaison with physical plant, recruitment/talent evaluation and team building, and performance reviews.

PORTFOLIO MANAGEMENT

Risk Analysis & Portfolio Construction, including selecting investment criteria and allocation/weighting methodology, identifying alpha and risk factors, conducting due diligence, preparing investment presentations; quantitative, correlation and concentration analysis; CAPM, APT, BARRA, simulation analysis, and distribution and cluster analysis. Portfolio building, including equity portfolios with different objectives, long/short, thematic and sector baskets, and structured notes, plus structured index, alternative investment and hedge fund vehicles; developing performance, exposure and risk monitoring and reporting systems.

PRODUCT MANAGEMENT

Package Goods Brand Management, including brand strategy development, positioning, advertising and promotion, PR, sales forecasting & P&L management, sales calls & consumer relations, cross-functional team building and management, and staff training.

PROJECT MANAGEMENT

Project Management, from project definition with stakeholders through deployment and closeout, including cost & risk analysis, work breakdown structures, scheduling and resource management, budgeting, communications planning, tracking & forecasting, contract compliance, change management, quality control, documentation and performance analysis, and reporting.

QUALITY

Quality Systems, including definition and alignment of organizational mission, vision, values, strategy, objectives, performance metrics, processes, policies, procedures, training, and communications; management review, control of documents and records, nonconformity investigation and root cause analysis, customer complaint management, performance monitoring and measurement, internal auditing and compliance, corrective and preventive action (CAPA), continual improvement; customer, supplier, and notified body liaison; and ISO 9001:20008 QMS registration. Compliance (Regulatory & Contract)–FDA Title 21 CFR, QSR, GxP, QbD, ICH, validation.

REAL ESTATE

Real Estate and Asset Management, including maintenance of all systems and services required to operate residential, commercial and retail facilities; planning for capital replacements and improvements; creating and administering budgets and accounting, directing maintenance staff and outside contractors; short- and long term planning, tenant mix and change of use, financing-all aspects, and labor relations.

RELATIONSHIP MANAGEMENT

Relationship Building, including referral solicitation programs, client services, private banking, new client relations programs, customer retention programs, and client special events: tennis outings, receptions, symposiums.

RESEARCH–BROKERAGE

Investment Selection, including making buy/hold/sell recommendations and decisions; identifying key factors and market opportunities, valuation and stock price movement through industry and competitive analysis, market research, and segmentation; identification of acquisition/investment candidates, analysis of key business and financial risks, financial statements, management letters and company documents; review of corporate objectives; site visits, field checks and management meetings.

SALES

Sales, including telephone and computer prospecting, scheduling appointments with decision-makers, defining customer needs, executive presentations and follow-up, contract negotiations, closing, key account management, time and territory management, and customer relations.

SCIENTIFIC

R&D Management, including overall research strategies; advancing drug discovery concepts to proof-of-concept—directing/monitoring target/lead selection and validation, pharmacological and pre-clinical evaluation of compounds to nominate development candidates and clinical indications-project planning, documentation, communication; creating and presenting "results packages" for attracting collaborators and pharmaceutical partners; collaborations with pharmaceutical partners; developing/maintaining intellectual property portfolio; government grant submissions; managing activities, allocation of efforts and budgets; and overseeing recruiting.

SELF-EMPLOYED / OWN BUSINESS

Operations Management, including budgeting & forecasts, cash management, sourcing & purchasing, merchandising, inventory control, staff training and daily supervision.

SOCIAL WORK

Community Human Services, including outreach into a community, conducting home visits and engaging clients into services, determining client's needs, assisting clients or groups to meet their needs within the context or constraints of the programs, attending collateral agency meetings with or on behalf of clients as required and advocating for clients, coaching, modeling, practicing skills or behavior, giving instruction, and case management and advocacy services to children and families in crisis.

SYSTEMS—LOW LEVEL

Release Management, including identifying and prioritizing the software release contents (i.e., new features and modification requests) across multiple products/services, synchronize the schedule across functional teams, issue resolution, facilitating release status meetings, and issuing Release Content Letters.

SYSTEMS

Information Technology (IT) Management, including identification of business needs/opportunities, advising senior management, selecting and designing systems architectures, developing and testing structured systems, developing & implementing cross-platform software release control systems, adopting enabling technologies, reengineering of functional work processes, and providing user training and support.

TAX

Tax Compliance & Planning, including international (Forms 1118, 5471, 5472, Subpart F, earnings & profits), federal (Forms 1120 & 1065), state income & franchise (separate company, combined & unitary returns), excise (Form 720), international planning (facility/office location, financing & tax/risk avoidance, foreign source income & tax credits), state planning (location, separate vs. combined), and excise planning (position holder rule, avoidance of double taxation).

TELECOMMUNICATIONS

Information Technology Management, including selecting and designing systems architectures, adopting enabling technologies, legacy systems replacement, make/buy decisions, developing, implementing and testing new applications, software test/quality assurance, hardware and software integration, systems installation and management, planning for asset protection, obsolescence avoidance, disaster recovery, establishing/monitoring SLAs and metrics, creating process flows, standards, best practice, documentation, and management reporting.

TRADING

Trading of financial markets in a proprietary manner, including monitoring market conditions, making markets, price discovery & negotiations, hedging, tracking market movements, developing models and trading strategies, as well as understanding the competitor's models and trading systems.

TRAINING

Training & Development, including gap analysis and needs assessments, evaluation of external training sources, selection of training principles and media, RFP & contracts in partnering ventures to control costs, train-the-trainer, customizing training programs and revisions; evaluating, selecting and working with graphic designers, printers, photographers and other suppliers through production; direction and supervision of freelancers and training vendors; conception, design and supervision of customized educational materials; production and distribution of educational materials (including web-based training, documentation, videos, newsletters, brochures, posters), logo development, designing informational websites and interactive tutorials; and public speaking.

TREASURY

Capital Structure & Funding, including assessment of cost of capital objectives, short-term versus long-term funding decisions, managing fixed and floating debt balances, cash forecasting, annual recommendations on dividend policy and level of stock buybacks, analysis and execution of funding strategies for potential acquisitions or divestitures, and relationship management.

TV-RADIO

Television Production, both live and video, including idea generation and consensus building, talent evaluation, daily site supervision and cost management, field producing, feature producing, graphics coordination, post-production activities, news gatherer, and continuous liaison with the sponsor/client.

WRITING & PUBLIC RELATIONS

Public Relations, including creating opportunities in print and broadcast national and trade media, pitching stories, presenting corporate strategy to industry analysts, investor relations, creative direction, media kits, trade shows, relationship building, identification of niche opportunities and forecasting, executive presentation and follow-up, preparation of proposals, closings, database management, client relations and partnership opportunities, product positioning, consumer contests and special events.

Weekly Column Writing, including initiating ideas, researching, developing source networks, selecting and covering appropriate events, following issues of concern to public officials, interfacing with public and government officials, monitoring competition's coverage and producing interesting columns each week.

* * *

Where Can a Person's Skills / Experience Be Employed?

Some years ago, I conceived a simple and inexpensive solution to this dilemma. This technique for evaluating possible employment opportunities was developed and appeared in a book I co-authored with Linda Kline, *Career Changing: The Worry-Free Guide*, published by Little, Brown & Co. in 1982. Called the Want-Ad Analysis Technique, it is used to define pertinent job content and other critical parameters for any job title.

The technique is simply a frequency analysis. Here's how it works. Collect a sample of 10 ads—all in the same job description, not job title—then do a frequency analysis of the elements in all the ads. Using the form below, the technique will quickly help you determine if you're qualified:

- to apply for any position
- what jargon you should use in your marketing resume
- which job accomplishments to emphasize
- what industries the job is in
- what job titles you might qualify for.

Try the technique. It will allow you to do career exploration right from the Internet.

WANT-AD ANALYSIS WORKSHEET

Ad Titles:				Ad Sources:	
1		5		1	
2		6		2	
3		7		3	
4		Industries Represented:			
# of Ads		1	4	7	

Ad Dates		2		5		8		
$ Range		3		6		9		

#	Job Requirements/ Skills/Education/Location	Frequency in Ads	# of Ads	%	Jargon
1					
2					
3					
4					
5					
6					
7					
8					
9					
10					
11					
12					
13					
14					
15					
16					
17					
18					

* * *

Reprinted from the *National Business Employment Weekly*

Packaging Yourself Like a Proven Product
Understand your customers and strive to meet their needs

By Lloyd Feinstein

Part One of Two

Job seekers often make the fatal mistake of thinking only about their own personal needs, not those of the hiring managers.

Putting an objective on a resume is a prime example of this self-centeredness. An objective represents your desires, not those of a hiring authority. The blunt truth is that employers don't care what you want. They're only interested in knowing if your skills will solve their problems and, hence, that you're the right person to fill an opening.

Unfortunately, as a job seeker, you aren't in a position to dictate your wishes. Until you learn to put employers' needs first and think like a hiring manager, the time, money and effort spent on your search is largely wasted.

Reorient your thinking by viewing your search as a classic sales problem. The hiring manger is the customer and you're the salesperson selling your ability to do a job and match the company's needs. Your problem is proving that ability. Like any salesperson, you must get your foot in the door (gain an interview) and close the sale (get a job offer) to earn your commission (salary).

John Gillespie, chief financial officer for Innovation Luggage Inc. in River Edge, N.J., says his attempts at job hunting were fruitless until he applied proven sales techniques.

"I failed to look at myself as a product during the early stages of my search," Mr. Gillespie says. "I was too close to the product to see myself objectively and, most of all, I lacked focus."

To resolve your sales problem and job hunt effectively, review some key concepts, then apply the sales and direct marketing techniques that follow.

Who's Your Customer?

To whom are you writing your resume and marketing letter? Find out before you prepare direct marketing materials, and heed the old Chinese saying, "If you don't know where you're going, any road will get you there!"

Rule out human resources as your customer, unless you want a position in that department. The best you can expect by writing to them is for your resume to be referred casually to some disinterested managers. The worst is that you'll be screened out immediately.

Instead, send your cover letter and resume to hiring managers who understand your role and potential and can relate to your accomplishments. To locate the names of such hiring "influences," review industry, company and professional directories at local libraries, or call the target company and ask who's in charge of the area that best fits your skills.

Packaging Yourself

Hiring authorities are impressed by candidates who, through their past achievements, demonstrate that they address current needs. To better understand how to package your work history, imagine you're a hiring manager with seven direct reports. One of these positions is vacant. To fill it, you, the

270

manager, must find a candidate with the necessary technical skills and the personality to mesh well with others in the department.

Personality, ironically, is the more important factor, representing as much as 75 percent to 80 percent of the hiring decision. This is because most hiring authorities are motivated by WIIFM, or "What's In It For Me?" and hiring a bad apple won't further their interests.

A 10-Second Window

By now, your hypothetical manager has received hundreds of resumes from potential candidates. To be selected, yours must show the benefits of hiring you, and that your personality matches that of other players. This is the crux of the job-search problem.

The first questions the manager needs answered are basic: Are you a job hopper? Has there been a steady progression in your job titles and responsibilities? Does this imply a commensurate increase in your salary? Clearly show on your resume the dates of previous employment, including titles held and key responsibilities. On average, it takes hiring managers about 10 seconds to scan a resume and form an opinion. Demonstrating steady career progression will help you over the first hurdle.

The next question the hiring manager wants answered is whether you can do the job and work well with others. This is best demonstrated through your previous accomplishments. Showing that you can resolve typical problems quickly and efficiently will prove that you're a committed team player.

Since your resume will be screened quickly, use an action-oriented "Problem-Action-Result" (PAR) format to convey your accomplishments. In short paragraphs highlighted by bullets, describe the following:

P: A problem you encountered (short phrase).

A: The action you took to resolve it. Use action verbs to describe what you did, not how you did it.

R: The results you achieved and the benefits to your employer. Use numbers, Percentages, or a short testimonial.

**Until you learn to think like a hiring manager,
the time, money and effort spent on your search is largely wasted**

The following are some typical accomplishments described using the PAR method:

For a financial executive:

- To reduce working capital investment, conceived and developed cash-control procedures. A/R and inventory reduction programs and monitoring systems. Result: achieved goals and reduced peak borrowing requirements by $3,100,000.

- To contain health-care costs, researched various carriers and programs, then negotiated various carriers and programs, then negotiated shift from a major medical plan to a combination HMO/CHP. Result: reduced annual costs to $80,486 from $90,672, saving 11.3%, expanded coverage to dental, reduced out-of-pocket employee expenses, and strengthened employee morale.

For a technical/back-office procession professional:

- To convert a government primary dealer's mortgage-backed securities business from a service bureau to a LAN system, trained personnel and managed a team to balance all front- and back-office management reports. Result: completed conversion in three weeks; converted client became full-time customer, and two other clients were recommended.

The PAR format is effective because it shows you're a problem-solver. If a hiring manager is faced with a challenge you've successfully resolved, your resume is likely to pique interest and an interview invitation.

Make sure, though, that you describe universal rather than specific problems when detailing your accomplishments. For example, senior financial executives can illustrate how their skills might transfer to another organization by describing how they resolved cash-flow management, financial reporting, accounting and MIS department discipline, cost control/reduction and other generic problems.

Mr. Gillespie credits the PAR technique for helping him to land his current position. He was hired after he used the PAR technique to rewrite his resume, which he sent in response to a classified ad. In addition to his full-time job, he runs a career counseling group in New Jersey for unemployed financial executives.

Showing that you can resolve typical problems quickly and efficiently will prove that you're a committed team player

"Once I learned to think like the hiring influence and use basic sales and marketing concepts in my job search, especially the use of PAR, the pieces all fell into place quickly," Mr. Gillespie says.

Finally, when writing your marketing materials, be enthusiastic. Effective salespeople encourage customers to buy by transferring their enthusiasm for their products. Since you're the product, you must believe in it completely. Otherwise, your best customers won't be interested.

Reprinted from the *National Business Employment Weekly*

How Direct Mail Can Excite Hiring Managers
Marketing letters are usually more effective than resumes
By Lloyd Feinstein

Editor's Note: In his article last week, Mr. Feinstein discussed the importance of viewing a job search like a sales problem with the hiring manager as customer, and you as the product and salesperson. He also described the Problem-Action-Result (PAR) method of illustrating accomplishments and experience in written marketing materials. This week, Mr. Feinstein explains how to prepare direct-mail letters that impress hiring managers.

Part II of II

The secret to landing new positions is showing future employers that it pays to hire you. Therefore, your marketing materials must "ring the cash register" by clearly demonstrating how an employer will benefit from giving you a job.

To be successful at this strategy, though, you must understand and emphasize hiring managers' needs, not your own. In other words, view your search like a sales campaign and think like your customers.

Since resumes often are ignored or returned to HR, it's wise to use effective marketing devices when communicating with hiring managers. The following is a guide to preparing marketing materials that interviewers are likely to read.

Getting Past Gatekeepers

When responding to classified ads, most job hunters are asked to send a resume, cover letter and salary history. Never send your salary history, though, since it's merely a personnel screening device. If your history doesn't match the range for the available position, you'll be eliminated.

But even if you send a resume and cover letter directly to a hiring manager, how do you know your materials will be read? Don't most executive assistants automatically send resumes to HR departments?

The solution to getting past executive assistants is to send a marketing letter that uses direct-mail principles. The following direct-mail formula developed by Richard C. Bordon, a New York University professor, is the basis for all U.S. advertising, including most of the junk mail you receive. It includes four elements:

1. The hook. A paragraph that describes the employer's greatest need.
2. Why you're mentioning it. This section typically starts with a sentence beginning with, "I am writing because…"
3. For instance. Additional paragraphs that describe your effectiveness and accomplishments. They should be bulleted or indented for emphasis, and match the employer's critical needs.
4. So what? What you want the reader to do, e.g., offer you an interview.

To prepare your marketing letters, review the accompanying sample. Since it's only one page, it's more likely to survive the executive assistant and be read by a busy hiring manager.

A Letter's Benefits

Note that the letter quickly answers the manager's first question, "What's in it for me?" by showing that the candidate can solve a pressing problem. Then, in the following paragraphs, the applicant explains how several generic problems were resolved. At the very least, managers view interviews as a way to gain free consulting advice. After receiving this letter, those who don't call to schedule a meeting are ignoring their own self-interest.

The letter also deliberately indicates the engineer's approximate age by including educational degree dates. Regardless of the age issue, however, hiring managers are likely to favor him because the letter answers critical hiring questions: Can the candidate do the job, solve pressing problems and help the employer save or make money?

Remember, the key is matching a target employer's greatest needs with your best accomplishments. Always emphasize and expand on the positive aspects of your work history, while reducing or eliminating any negatives that might work against you in the hiring process. Your ultimate goal is to gain an interview invitation. If the interviewer then determines that your personality fits the organization, you may be offered a position. Always emphasize the positive aspects of your work history while eliminating any negatives.

Finally, since different managers have unique needs, create several versions of your letter by reconstructing and adjusting the paragraphs.

The beauty of a well-written marketing letter is that it serves as a functional resume without actually being one. It shows off your most impressive career achievements, but not necessarily in order or at only one employer. For instance, each of the problems the engineer solved could have occurred at different companies.

There's no doubt that marketing letters are effective. I used one to change from a training and HR position with a nonprofit hospital to a training management job with Cadence Industries Corp., a for-profit $120 million diversified company in West Caldwell, N.J.

When the position was advertised, I sent a letter to the manager specified in the ad. I later interviewed with David Balaban, then director of human resources at Cadence, and now senior vice president with Daniel Silverstein Associates, an executive search firm in East Brunswick, N.J. Mr. Balaban said recently that he thought I had sent him a resume. Instead, the letter alone was the basis for my interviews with Cadence managers and my subsequent hire.

Although I didn't need a resume to land my Cadence job, most hiring managers aren't comfortable scheduling an interview until they receive one. Use similar Problem-Action-Results statements on your resume, but don't send it to the hiring manager. Too often, extraneous resume information that doesn't relate to the employer's immediate needs can be used to screen you out. Instead, bring your resume to the meeting and emphasize how your accomplishments fit the employer's objectives. Also, try to demonstrate that your personality and style fit that of the current management team. Unfortunately, in any job market, the most successful candidates are those who are perceived as the most qualified, even if that isn't the case. You may be the best candidate, so use a customer-oriented approach to your job search to ensure that you're viewed that way.

Sample Action Letter—for a heating/ventilation/air conditioning chief engineer

Hiring Manager
Title
Company
Street
City, State, ZIP code

Dear _____ :

To reduce fumes in a 750,000 sq. ft. municipal garage, I added direct gas-fired burners to the rooftop package instead of putting a large number of indirect gas-fired furnaces on the large energy recovery system. Result: eliminated the need to add 200 inches to each of 12 rooftop packages; saved $20,400 per unit (total savings of $244,800); and reduced the overall length of each package to 20' to 36'.

I am writing because your organization may need a profit-oriented engineering professional with my background and experience. I am currently vice president of engineering for a $13 million division of a large, privately held industrial corporation. You may find the following accomplishments of interest.

- To stay competitive while maintaining the integrity of our product lines and profit margins, I demonstrated the salient features of our equipment and how they compared with competing products to consulting engineers and customers. Designed special features into our products to "lock out" our competitors. Result: convinced customers that our products, and field service repairs, if necessary, were superior; over a five-year period, 52% of all bids were successfully converted into sales orders. This represented 25% of the company's business during this period.

- To reduce costs associated with the fabrication of our product lines, I assessed our products using value-analysis techniques. Made extensive structural design changes, reduced assembly-time labor costs, and employed commonality of parts. Result: after two years, contributed more than $200,000 toward the profit base of $315,000 that year; direct contributions to profits have continued to be realized over the last two years.

- To satisfy top management's, internal sales' and the manufacturing department's requests for design drawings on a timely basis, I interviewed managers and supervisors, then created and

277

implemented a priority system to log and track requests. Established priorities based on customer delivery requirements, and color-coded orders for quick identification. Result: turn-around time reduced to two weeks from four weeks; eliminated one- to-four-week delay caused by the credit department.

- Interviewed, hired and trained a graduating engineer. After a three-year period, he was promoted to chief engineer in charge of bills of material and applications.

I have received my MME from Stevens in 1974 and a ME from Stevens in 1963. My salary requirements are competitive. I will call you in a few days to make an appointment for us to discuss my experience further in a personal interview.

Very truly yours,

14206422R00155

Printed in Great Britain
by Amazon.co.uk, Ltd.,
Marston Gate.